the field

the field

Victoria Garza

JACKLEG PRESS

JackLeg Press
www.jacklegpress.org

Copyright © 2022 by Victoria Garza. Published 2022 by JackLeg Press. All
rights reserved.
Printed in the United States of America.

ISBN: 978-1-7375134-9-0

Library of Congress Control Number: 2022936413

Cover design by Jennifer Harris & Jay Snodgrass
Cover image: Kiss Joy by Kimi Eisele

Dedication

This book is dedicated to my mother, Maria Teresa Garza, who taught me that there is a correct way to begin things, a correct way to end things, and a correct way to continue on.

Prologue

In the northern provinces of Argentina, they don't weep for the death of small children. One less mouth on earth, one more angel in heaven. Death is drunk and dances from the first cock crow, sucking in long draughts of carob-bean liquor and chichi to the rhythm of bass drum and guitar. While the dancers whirl and stomp their feet, the child is passed from arm to arm. Once the child has been well rocked and fully celebrated, everyone breaks into song to start it on its flight to Paradise. There goes the little traveler, clothed in its Sunday best, as the song swells; and they bid it farewell, setting off fireworks, taking great care not to burn its wings.

—Felix Coluccio, *Dictionario Folklorico Argentino*

Sonya, Michael, Christopher — Tía Patricia

Jamie, Jessica — Tía Maria

Tío Ed — Jason, Joshua, Renae, Dallas, Eddie

Rachel, Frank — Tía Eva

Tío Martin — Jason

Samuel, Christina — Tía Lupita

Tío John — Hope, Faith, Jennifer, Corey, Jacob, Janelle, Alejandra

Peggy, Joe, Eddie, **Connie**, Israel — Tía Maggie

Tío Joe — Joey, Jarrod, Alena

Victoria, **Virginia** — Teresa (Mom)

Tío Gil — Gil, Tony, Tanya

Marcelino (Grandfather)
Manuela (Grandmother)

Jesse (Dad)

Gilbrando (Grandfather)

Emilia (Grandmother)

Partial Family Tree

1.

Left behind
and drenched as the grass,
   with drops of dew.

Kobayashi Issa

In the middle of what looks like a field, right next to Interstate 280
South in northern Ohio, is a grave. It's a new cemetery, with few trees
and fewer graves. On the ground is a rectangular granite stone that
reads Virginia Marie Garza, Born October 31, 1968, Died May 19,
1978. My nine-year-old sister and cousin were put in the ground
forever. I was ten and not having any idea how long forever was, I was
constantly surprised. And still, I am surprised.

I don't know what to call this story.

For three weeks and two days after my sister's death, I am terrified of dying.
I am terrified that I or my parents or my grandparents or the dog across the
street will die. Having decided I was barely surviving, I decided I was a Jew

and hiding in Ohio. When I suggested this to my mother, she gently asked me how I could manage to be a Catholic and a Jew at the same time. I reminded her that the early Christians were Jews and so was Jesus Christ. "Yes, that's true," she says while stopping me from pulling a loose thread from her brown and orange flowered bedspread. I tell my mother all about Anne Frank and remind her that some people can be hiding for years when everyone thinks they are dead—but they are not, they're just hiding. My mother reminds me that my sister is not hiding.

Saying "I know she's dead, Mom" does not prevent me from thinking that my sister is just hiding and bound to show up at any moment, and I should therefore be prepared. Thus, began my love of lists. As long as I could list my thoughts, I felt a degree of control over them, as if by listing them I was slapping my thoughts into submission. My most important list was a series of questions I would ask my sister upon her return home.

Question number 1: What is the color blue?

Question number 2: Is it true for sure that my dreams are not real?

Question number 3: If yes to number 2, then why do we dream?

Question number 4: Can you read my thoughts?

Question number 5: If yes to number 4, then what exactly are thoughts?

Question number 6: Where did you go?

Question number 7: Is there really a God?

Question number 8: If yes to number 7, then what is God really like?

Question number 9: Did God tell you that I told him to tell you that I love you?

Question number 10: Do you have super-human powers since you took your trip?

Question number 11: If yes to number 10, then make a list and teach me your powers. If no, then what is the point of meeting God?

The relief I feel from performing such an exercise is so profound that it consistently overshadows the knowledge that she is not coming back. Rather than adding to my list, I am always changing it. I always choose eleven items, one number shy of my favorite number. There was some logic to this, but I can't remember what it was. Maybe it's the same logic my cousin Rachel (whose pajama party my sister and cousin never arrived at) used when she decided to skip her birthday in 1978. We found out a year later when Rachel announced to everyone's surprise that she was a year younger than she actually was. She said, matter-of-factly, "I skipped that year." I skipped weeks and months after Gina's death. I just wiped them off the map of time. And then I took to daydreaming without realizing it, skipping time altogether. Anything could set me off. I could fall into a trance while looking at a beetle behind the garage. When I finally heard my mother calling me, I had no way of explaining to her what I was doing. I couldn't say, "I was looking at a beetle," because that would sound stupid. So, I yelled back, "Nothing," which my mother, like all mothers, took to mean that I was doing something I shouldn't have been doing.

Death does that to time, compresses it, slows it down until time ceases to exist. A year feels like a week, three years, like three weeks. Carlos Castañeda's Don Juan says that death lives behind you to your left, an arm's stretch away—ready to tap you on the shoulder. Lorca calls it duende, death as friend, death as companion.

But then there is my "other" feeling.

At the funeral, I walk into the field adjacent to the parking lot. I close my eyes and the blazing sun behind my eyeballs lifts me out of the parking lot and into Pearson Park. From there I can see Pickle Road, the truck, the field, and my sister, but instead of her lying there dead, she sits lotus-style eating an orange. It came to be that I could see anything I wanted by closing my eyelids. The point wasn't to not use the eyes; the point was to close the eyelids. The day I flew from the parking lot to the field at Pickle Road was the day I was introduced to my "other" feeling, Grace. Grace is Aretha Franklin. She wears a white gown, with diamonds for eyes and snow-white hair. She is magic. She is the sun, the fresh-cut grass, and the smell of dirt. She is the smile on my face and the calmness in my heart and all of this on what turned out to be, still, the worst day of my life.

Grace resides to my right, and she is louder and far more beautiful and more powerful than death and therefore capable of coaxing death to do whatever she wants. She is powerful enough to make death shut up. Death would whisper, "Certainly, if it can happen to you, it can happen to anyone—or worse yet, it can happen to you again," but then Grace would whisper, "Yes, my girl, it is not only true, but it is The Truth, so why worry about it?" So instead, three weeks and two days after my sister's death, I decide I want to die. I imagine my death in hundreds of ways. I die riding my bike, smashed to a pulp by a reckless teenager who only has his driver's permit. I die drowning in dirty Lake Erie after jumping off the jetty. I freeze to death outside my bedroom window from eating too much snow. I get struck by lightning. I die when I fall out of a tree and crack my head open, and instead of blood pouring out there are just dead thoughts that trickle out and collect in a puddle, which I then stomp on and watch scatter in the wind. However, thinking I finally understand what an attack of the heart means, I decide to die of a heart attack. Except in the case of my heart, I decide it will not give me any warnings—it will just beat slower and slower until it stops, like melting an ice cube under my armpit in the middle of summer—slowly or quickly my heart starts shrinking until I see it's the size of a pinhead beating tiny beats, like a lighthouse beam, flowing through my bloodstream, working its way out of me through my eyeball and then flying away. My heart waves to myself, dead down there in the yard.

2.

But day doth daily draw my sorrows longer,
And night doth nightly make grief's strength
seem stronger.

William Shakespeare, *Sonnet XXVIII*

I look forward to sleep. I look forward to the intoxicating blanket of a consciousness that allows her to be alive. So alive, in fact, that every morning upon waking, in that in-between state, I would forget my sister was dead. And was surprised again when death would stab me awake. A year went by before I could remember one nice thing I'd done for her. For a year, I was terrified that I had never been nice to her. It seems impossible to feel good by looking at my life as it appears to be in this moment. After closing my eyes and imagining the world as I want it to be, I slowly begin to construct a different feeling. It's quite surprising, really. It's not happiness. It's something else.

May 19, 1978. It is springtime in Ohio, where the air smells like moist dirt and fresh-cut grass, something like my sister's mud pies.

My uncle forgets something and drives back to the house; I jump out of the truck because my favorite uncle, Ed, has just arrived. Football or pajama party? I choose football. It's the last time I see her, my little sister Virginia, whom we call Gina. She waves from the back of the truck, close to the cab, where it is safe. She smiles and shakes her head a little, the way she does to get her hair out of her face. She is sitting next to Connie, our cousin, two little girls going to a pajama party on a sunny late afternoon in May. My aunt Patricia and my cousin Peggy are going to be chaperones. They are in the truck. They and my uncle survive.

I am wearing dark green slacks with a small flair at the bottom and a blouse that looks like a Pollack painting with a large collar, my favorite outfit. On the day of the funeral, like most, I have permission to wear whatever I want. I am wearing the brightest outfit of anyone. I get up from my father's lap and proceed to make my way to the back of the funeral parlor. I let people hug me because I know it makes them feel better. The funeral home is packed, and I have to make it through a lot of hands touching my shoulders, looking at me with crazy, sympathetic eyes. But I can't feel a thing and I don't want to act inappropriately, so I just keep my head down and walk. I take small steps. When I reach the foyer, I sneak out of the funeral home into the sunlight. I am facing a parking lot full of shiny cars surrounded by endless acres of farmland. For the first time in my short life, I really take notice of the sun and don't take for granted a single thing. I feel the sun on my face, and it feels warm like I'm glowing from the inside out. I take a deep breath and for one luxurious moment, I am alone and swollen with relief. I feel grateful—for what, I have no idea.

There are only a few things I remember about the wake and fewer things about the funeral. I remember my dad's lap, the feeling of holding him up even though he was sitting down. I remember his shoes, Gina's picture on the closed casket (and not the picture I would've chosen), my mother standing strongly for the endless line of well-wishers, and the small wooden cross Nancy's oldest son put inside the palm of my hand, and the packed room and the saturated sweet smell of women's perfume. I remember resisting the urge to double-check if she is actually dead. I fixate on the casket, thinking, I should just lift it up and see for myself. I remember the parking lot. I remember the old dead lady in the empty room next door. I peeked in and thought how nice it would be if we could all share since we needed the space and it looked like she needed some people.

This is when I started hiding.

At ten years old, my mind wanders, it gets confused and then it just gets real tired. One minute I'm sitting between my grandparents thinking about what my sister and I will get to eat for dinner, and the next minute, the back of the hearse opens its jaws and I watch them shove her casket in. My sister is dead, I almost forgot. No dinner, or lunch or breakfast, ever. And I think to myself that we are only halfway done. Next, we'll place her in the ground and...

I know the drill. In my grandmother Emilia's care, we attended plenty of funerals. In fact, for some time I was convinced that people only died in summer. We would follow the cars with flags on them in a long line and go to what looked like a very pretty park while my grandmother explained the complicated web that led her to know someone who knew someone who knew the person who died. Then we'd watch them put a long box in the ground, and I would try not to cry for everyone's loss while my sister would cry as if she knew the deceased intimately. Then we'd go to Burger Chef for a cheeseburger and fries and a chocolate milkshake. Gina would get a fish sandwich with cheese and a strawberry milkshake. My thoughts keep getting jumbled up. I simply cannot get my mind to behave—I know I won't be going to Burger Chef after this funeral, and then I feel guilty for having Burger Chef thoughts in the first place.

The morning after the funeral, I try to eat my cereal and she's not sitting there. I go to brush my teeth, and for the first time, I have the sink to myself. What are we going to do with her pink toothbrush? Why didn't anyone think of it? This seems to me in this moment a very serious error. I'm terrified of my bus driver asking me where she is; maybe she didn't hear the news. What will I say? I imagine it so vividly that when I get on the bus, I hear myself saying, "She's dead," and walk to the very last seat. I don't want anyone watching me. Kids don't want to sit with the sister of the dead girl, except for my sister, who would sit with anyone to make him or her feel better. I imagine her smiling and saying, "It's okay that I'm dead, everything is going to be alright."

I dream that my mother and I are walking down Howard Road, away from our house. She is holding my hand. I'm crying. I keep looking back. But we're leaving her behind, I say. My mother tugs on my arm. She's not there, Mija, we have to keep going. Charcoal clouds are hanging low as my mother leads me into my future.

3.

If you want to know why you cannot reach your own beautiful ideas. If you reach instead the edge of the thinkable, which leaks.

Anne Carson, *Decreation*

October 2001. I'm driving alone on the Brooklyn Queens Expressway, returning home to the city, and the skyline has a big hole in it. It occurs to me that everyone I know and everyone I don't know will die. I was in a small Texas town when it happened. It's the kind of Texas that reminds you of Sam Shephard's short stories—intricate, detailed, and hot, with a minimal mundane beauty only because it is so unselfconscious. The town is called Orange Grove, and although I've never noticed any groves, there are convenience stores and trucking equipment companies, and oil-rig supply stores scattered around town.

I take the off-ramp onto Flatbush Avenue and pass twenty-five two-ton trucks filled with debris sitting on the Brooklyn side of the Manhattan Bridge. I am hauling the world up Park Slope steps; nothing is the same. I sit on my favorite chair in the dining room and immediately notice the ash on the windowsill. In fact, there is dust and ash everywhere, on everything. An avalanche sets off in my heart.

Just a week earlier, when I was in Texas visiting my grandparents, taking long slow walks through long slow days, I reminded myself that these people around me are mine and I'm theirs, and it's true that if I had known when I was ten that one of four noble truths is "suffering is caused by attachment," I may have been inclined to detach.

Fall of 1987, when I am nineteen, I see her again for the first time since the accident. I am waiting for her at my childhood home, my mother telling me to be patient, and my entire extended family in the backyard having a barbecue. My father drives up in Apa Chele's white Chevy pickup truck, the one with the blue cap. My sister climbs out from the back. I race out the front screen door and hear it slam behind me, as it had always done, coiled noises that died down quickly till the door was still, open. My mother would yell at us for not taking the extra second to securely close it: "You are letting the flies in. How many times do I have to tell you girls?" We would be halfway across the yard when one of us would remember and stop cold and have to run back and click the screen door shut before my mom noticed. My sister is four years old, barely able to fit her tummy into her striped polyester tank top, and she is, as she has always been, barefoot. She hugs me, and for a moment I think it's my long-lost friend Grace. We go inside the house and into a room that never existed off the kitchen where the phone is, next to the toaster and the dining room table. My mother used to call us from that window. She would sit on a chair just close enough to talk on the mustard-yellow telephone with the over-stretched cord and smoke a cigarette in private so she could blow the smoke out the window while keeping an eye on us playing in the yard. My mother, at the height of her maternal power in my young mind, is always thirty-three years old. She moves quickly through the world, juggling two young girls, a 9 to 5 job at the Ohio State Welfare Agency, close ties to our church, guitar practice, and being the eldest daughter of a large Mexican American family. My mother was organized and efficient. She could change the oil on our car, fix the furnace when it was acting up, and sew stitches on my favorite T-shirt. After my parents divorced, we operated as a team of three, with just enough chores and responsibilities to make us feel like we were making an important contribution to the family machine, but not so many that we were burdened by how little money we had.

Through the window is now a bare room, a bare mattress on a solitary twin bed, an old one, high off the ground. My sister sits dangling her legs. The bed stands between two tall narrow church windows that reach the ceiling: beams of white light too bright to look at scatter molecules of dust and lint. This is the way people imagine this when the dead come to visit, I thought. Something Godly is about to happen.

Before I can turn to face her, she tells me without speaking that it is time to let her go; the accident was not my fault, and she is not going to be able to stay. I don't feel angry, nor do I realize, until that moment, that I felt guilty for being alive. When I turn around and she is gone, just like that, I cannot say I feel better for the visit. I feel lucky, but always I feel there is no time for me to tell her things. I have no idea what I would say. Maybe I would tell her how sorry I am for teasing her, for saying she was such a baby for crying over the television news, for taking a bigger portion of ice cream, for being embarrassed that I had to take her wherever I went, for making her beg to sleep with me at night when she was afraid of the shadows, for being so cranky when she was so cheerful. I awake sweaty and sobbing in my college dorm room.

Maybe, just maybe, the accident wasn't my fault after all.

At the age of twenty, I decided I am a survivor, which has the distinct flavor of making me feel like a refugee, someone who has barely escaped death and other unimaginable atrocities, but who is now living in a foreign country with the good fortune of going to college to make something of myself. Why am I alive and my sister and cousin are dead?

"Shankara, Freud, and Jiminy Cricket all agree, a dream is a wish your heart makes when you're fast asleep," suggests Ken Wilber in *One Taste.*

I left New York City permanently in April 2002. Leaving felt like a betrayal, I was turning my back on it during its time of need. Apathy towards one's life after a catastrophe like 9/11 provided me clues about the violence of despair. I imagine that in a state of war or chaos, as in all things crucial and pending, the meaning of life, as it is lived daily, is more comprehensible. The important matters weed themselves out and one is left with the essential nature of one's love. My shit was packed and heading for Los Angeles.

What I thought was real was not solid. *The Tibetan Book of the Dead* says,

Anyone can die at any time in any place. Our sense of the concreteness of the life situation, of the solidity of the waking world of the five senses and their objects, is a complete error. Nothing that we think we are, do, feel, or have has any essence, substance, stability, or solidity. All the somethings in and around us with which we preoccupy ourselves from morning to night are potentially nothing to us. If we died, they would dissolve in our tightest grasp.

Life is not a solid fact.

4.

No one behind, no one ahead.
The path the ancients cleared has closed.
And the other path, everyone's path,
easy and wide, goes nowhere.
I am alone and find my way.

Octavio Paz, *The Tradition*

I am the God Helios, driving the sun, my chariot across the sky. I see
the heat waves rising from the dirt road ahead of me. We turn onto a
county road. My cousin Julie taps me on the shoulder, "We should
get back or Ama Mela is going to worry!" I pretend I don't hear her.
Something peculiar comes over me, something I haven't felt for a
long time. It's elation, and a bewildering, blistering freedom. This is
the first summer I remember enjoying after my sister's death. I am
twelve years old. My dad is in San Antonio, and I am spending the
afternoon at "el rancho," which is what my dad's parents call their
modular home and five acres of land they acquired to retire on. I
holler to the side so my cousin Julie can hear me say, "I want to ride

off right into the sun." "But we should tell Ama first," she screams back. When I come back to my senses, I manage to turn around the dirt bike that is too tall for me, and back we go. Julie suggests we take a shortcut once we get close to el rancho. She points, I go.

I realize too late that I'm heading straight into a new (meaning tight) barbed wire fence way too fast. At the last second, I close my eyes and brace my arms. Julie screams as the front tire barely makes it underneath the lowest wire and the other wires make contact with me and pull me off the bike. Julie and the bike end up on the other side of the fence. The back tire is ripping off the flesh on her thigh. I hear her faintly in the background when I slowly open one blurry eye and have a macro lens view of nothing but dirt. I think to myself how much I love the smell of Texas, a mixture of dirt, large animals, and dried grass, and how if I died right now, how grateful I'd feel to have experienced the sun kissing my face again. I imagine my sister's small, bare feet. I imagine myself reaching for the bike to turn it off, but I can't move my body. The motor stops. Blurry, Julie wiggles away from the bike when I feel these big arms pick me up off the ground. I hear my grandmother screaming in Spanish as she flies out of her house across the street. She's having a panic attack again; I think to myself. Julie limps behind the man who's carrying me, and I look back at her and start laughing. We're both cackling uncontrollably—we're alive!

The man places me softly on the couch, and my grandmother hurries to the bathroom to get ointments and a washcloth. I tell her not to bother, "Relax, Ama, we're not dead." It is the most fun I can remember having in a long time. "You should've seen the sun, Ama—tell her Julie, it was unbelievable," and on and on until five minutes pass and our laughter disappears. The pain has arrived with such acuteness I can't help but start crying. I have a deep barb cut that stretches the cross length of my neck and chest and picks up again across my arm. I have one swollen bloody eyeball with a barb scratch from the corner of my eyelid to my ear. My nostril has been clipped from the rest of my nose.

"Off with the clothes," says my grandmother, as she starts taking off my shirt. It hurts me, but she doesn't care right now, she is focused and upset. I hide my pain so as not to upset her further, and I look at Julie and shrug my shoulders. Ama Mela goes on in Spanish about how people lose their heads in Texas, literally, from barbwire fence accidents. "They get decapacitated!" I never correct her English. She smells good, always, a mixture of old-lady perfume and talcum powder. Ama Mela calls Apa Chele and tells him to get home—the girls must go to the hospital, "por si acaso se rompió algo" (in case something got broken). And then she has to call my mom, which I know she doesn't want to do. She does not want to provide further proof to my mother that my father, who is nowhere in the vicinity, is totally irresponsible.

My mother stands across from me watching the doctors put an orange liquid all over my cuts and abrasions. I watch her with one eye as they patch the other one. It's the first time I feel how scary it must be for her. She controls her fear with a quiet, firm silence. She is not pleased with me, but she is too relieved to scold me. "You should've seen it, Mom. It was the most beautiful thing ever." My mother sees me. Maybe she remembers finding me in the field next to the funeral home, with my wet eyes closed and my face pressed towards the sky, because I see her face soften.

February 29, 2008, Corpus Christi, Texas. My grandfather on my father's side, Marcelino Garza, died of a heart attack. He was eighty-three years old. He was born on February 25, 1925, in Yorktown, Texas, to Tomás Garza and Teodala Salinas Garza. My grandmother is sitting on my dad's bed, explaining to her neighbor, a short brown weathered man who works in the oil fields that the lanky girl, the one "con todo brazos y piernas" (with all arms and legs) he picked up off the ground so many years ago is now the woman standing in front of him. He is paying his respects to the memory of my dead grandfather by talking about old times. He grins wide shaking his head in disbelief. My grandmother tells me they didn't know each other before then—that they became good friends after that day he picked me off the ground. Tío.

The official obituary is summed up as follows: He was employed as a roofer with J.P. Morrow Roofing and Sheet Metal Company. He was later employed as an air conditioning technician with York Air Conditioning Company until his retirement. He was a U.S. Navy veteran of World War II. He is survived by four daughters, my Tías Andrea, Julie, Janey, and Nora; and two sons, my father, and my uncle Marcelino Jr.; one brother Tomás Jr.; and three sisters, Eloisa, Petra, and Maria; sixteen grandchildren; forty-three great-grandchildren; and seven great-great-grandchildren. That is supposed to sum him up. What it doesn't say is that he was a very kind, quiet man who worked really hard his entire life with none of the traditional symbols to show for it. He spoke little to no English, although he seemed to understand his Midwestern granddaughters who spoke little to no Spanish perfectly well. In the sweltering Texas summers, he wore one of several Halliburton baseball caps and an open work shirt with maybe just one button fastened. His belly would hang over his trousers, and he'd drink a beer while mowing the lawn. He had enormous hands. At night, he'd make a huge fire in the fire pit and welcome any visitors, mostly his sons-in-law, to join him in a beer and some conversation. As his hearing got worse, one could see him recede into his own world more and more.

I touch Apa Chele's hands. They are cool. His lips are pursed tightly in an expression he's never worn in his life. He is wearing nice black wranglers, a crisp white shirt, a black leather vest, and a bolo tie. There is a black and red strand of rosary beads in his thick, large hands. His black cowboy hat sits inside the coffin. I take a real good look at him, and I notice a tiny little stain near the cuff of his shirt. I don't know why I smile, but it seems to me the only real thing left of him. I'm reminded that life is messy and for those of us who want to live, a messy life is better than no life at all.

I dream my mother is driving our dark green Fiat convertible down a deserted road. It's remote and the landscape barren. I say I want to drive off the end of the world. She says that would be impossible and fruitless. I can't imagine a world without fruit.

5.

The anesthetizing influence of habit having ceased, I would begin to have thoughts, and feelings, and they are such sad things.

Marcel Proust, *Swann's Way*

To make matters simple for myself (because it's hard to be ten years old and have suspicions about God), I began my longstanding fascination with spirituality. I told my progressive Catholic mother there is something seriously wrong with this idea. What idea, she asks. God, I say. This is when I decided I was not only a Jew and a Catholic, but the goddess Athena, as well, all rolled into one. A true spiritual warrior dedicated to destroying any ignorance that impedes the expression of the truth. I was the protector of civilization. Thus, I began my spiritual period, which was characterized by an increasing love of solitude. Aside from my mom, everyone else annoyed me. I would spend hours reading all things related to God. I was particularly interested in the saints, and their peculiar or eccentric lives. I loved the scholarship of St. Augustine (although I understood very little of anything he said) and the devotion to an experiential knowledge of God that seemed to absorb St. Teresa of Avila (it helped that my mother was named after this saint). I loved St. Francis of Assisi for his love of animals. And I loved the Gospel According to Peanuts, with a cover of Snoopy kneeling in prayer on top of his red doghouse. I was in need of a spiritual vocabulary, so I stole phrases and words to give life to my feelings. For example, I learned that St. Teresa could barely bring herself to have conversations.

Sometimes it gives me great pain to have to have dealings with others, it afflicts me so much that it causes me to weep profusely, because all my longing is to be alone.

She goes on...

If I speak or have dealings with some secular persons because matters can't be otherwise, and even though the subject may concern prayer, I find if the conversation is prolonged, just a diversion and unnecessary, I am forcing myself to continue, because such conversation is a severe hardship for me. Amusements that I used to like, and things of the world all annoy me; and I cannot look at them.

I felt like I had a great deal in common with St. Teresa. I could no longer ride my bike in the garage, an activity I once took pleasure in, precisely because I was not supposed to do it. It was forbidden once I crashed my bike on the concrete floor while trying to ride in circles around a steel pole in the center of the garage. I showed up in my second-grade class the next morning and Mrs. Schmidt took a look at the large bump on my neck the size of a goiter. She called my mother who then felt guilty that she had not noticed this on my neck that very morning. I could no longer bring myself to chase down the ice cream truck, or go exploring in the woods behind our house, or listen to ABBA on my collapsible turntable stereo or eat the snow outside my window. I began to enjoy reading and writing precisely because it allowed me to be in my own world, away from everyone else. I was given to creating long titles of my works like the ones peculiar to the period in which St. Teresa lived. The first edition of the saint's works, published in Salamanca in 1588, was called *Meditations or exclamations of the soul to God written by Mother Teresa of Jesus in the year 1569 on different days according to the spirit our Lord gave her after Communion.* My titles went something like, Meditations or confusing conversations with God written by Victoria Garza in the year 1978 on different winter evenings while contemplating life and death questions beyond her control and about which she knows nothing.

It was an investigative period, too. My mother was constantly fielding questions, having to explain the inadequacies and contradictions of her religion. "Are gay people going to hell?" I'd ask. My mother's eyes would widen in disbelief. "Of course not, Mija! What would make you think that?" "The Pope doesn't like gay people and Jews don't believe in Jesus. My friend is Jewish, and she said she is gay." "No, no, no, no. No one is going to hell. Your friend is a wonderful person and God doesn't care about that, and he doesn't care what religion or culture you're from," my mother would sigh heavily.

Apparently, there were lots of little details the Catholic Church cared about that God didn't.

In our home, there was never a shortage of books about the saints or the Father, Son, or Holy Ghost. I enjoyed an entire winter during my spiritual period listening to my mother's Jonathon Livingston Seagull album and hypothesizing all the ways my life was exactly like the saints'. This list I called, "The Accumulation of the Miraculous as a Way to Get Rid of Bad Thoughts."

If I concentrated all my efforts on the tiniest things, for example, taking out the trash for my Tía Lupe, folding the clothes, getting the mail... then one day, those things would grow until one day life meant something else. I would be made of all the nice stuff I'd done for people. The Daishonin writes," If you light a lantern for another, it will also brighten your own way." So, I started lighting lanterns because it was not something that could be entrusted to a God who was not concerned with details.

11 LANTERNS TO GET RID OF BAD THOUGHTS

Lantern number one: I did not hide in the attic of the garage today.

Lantern number two: I was not grumpy at breakfast even though my mother tells me I'm just not a morning person and there's no use feeling bad about it.

Lantern number three: I alphabetized my mother's albums and 8-tracks.

Lantern number four: I mowed my Tía Lupe's yard.

Lantern number five: I stopped counting my steps for an entire day.

Lantern number six: I wrote dad a letter without asking for money even though mom wanted me to ask for the child support.

Lantern number seven: I helped my grandmother hang the clothes on the line.

Lantern number eight: I wrote two extra book reports for Mrs. Keith.

Lantern number nine: I made a card for my bus driver.

Lantern number ten: I finally helped my mother with her puzzle of a winter cabin near a babbling brook.

Lantern number eleven: I prayed to Grace using my own words and not the ones I had memorized.

What I didn't plan for, however, was the realization that the very same good thoughts can instantly turn bad and vice versa. One year after her death, I was changing the sheets on my bed. I had tiny blue flower print sheets while she had yellow. She had a yellow room with two windows, and I had a baby blue room with two windows and a connecting playroom that became my office, equipped with an old record player, desk, bookshelves my dad built, and a dark cork board above my desk to pin up all my important things. My window faced west and opened onto a small roof, and from the street, one could see my window on the right and her window on the left. The lamppost in front of our house dangled rusty black metal numbers, 853 for 853 Howard Road, Curtice, Ohio. In summer, we'd crawl over my bed and out my window to look at the stars. In winter, we'd reach out and scoop snow into our mouths while still tucked in my bed. My sister put her foot over mine. Always my bed, always my window.

I fanned the sheet above my head and watched it settle on top of her (she's gone one instant and there the next). She giggled uncontrollably as I pretended to be annoyed. When I fanned the sheet up in the air, the day was bright and sunny, and I could hear my mother playing Neil Diamond downstairs. Everything was fine, I was happy; spring had come again. When the sheet settled on my empty bed, I began to sob, heartbroken. How so quickly and so completely could my bright day turn dark? My mother, with her usual telepathy, appeared at my door. We sat together on my bed, the sheet in my mouth and the wind blowing through my window. The street, the window, and snow in summer and me on my bed with my mother, both of us without her.

Virtually everyone who has ever experienced grief describes this phenomenon as "waves." In *The Year of Magical Thinking*, Joan Didion explains that "grief has no distance. It comes in waves, paroxysms, and sudden apprehensions that weaken the knees, blind the eyes and obliterate the dailiness of life." In quoting a physician's manual she adds:

> Sensations of somatic distress occurring in waves lasting from twenty minutes to an hour at a time, a feeling of tightness in the throat, choking with shortness of breath, need for sighing and an empty feeling in the abdomen, lack of muscular power, and an intense subjective distress described as a tension or mental pain.

The physical sensations are an ambush. They sneak up on you, sucker punch you in the face. One minute I'm fine, and the next minute I'm sobbing. I feel disoriented as if lost in a huge department store and they're turning off all the lights and closing up before I've had a chance to find my mother. But I can't scream out. For some inexplicable reason, it's as if what is happening to me is my fault, and I don't want to bring attention to myself. It's the prolonged moment(s) when I don't want to admit that there is something wrong; meanwhile, the world is clearly not operating according to my expectations, but I don't want to embarrass myself by mentioning it.

So I watch myself watching myself, silently.

The only beauty I can imagine in losing someone when you are a child is the mere fact that you have no intellectual power over any of the sensations. The feelings of sadness, loneliness, anger, anxiety, or lack of interest in all the things that used to make you joyful become the veil over your life. You accept them more readily. You are more adept in the present moment and have not yet cultivated the techniques used to mask your true feelings.

That happens later.

The Mayo Foundation for Medical Education and Research explains in surprising detail that memories and emotions rekindled through reminders are called anniversary reactions. Anniversary reactions can also evoke powerful emotional memories, experiences in which you vividly recall the feelings and events surrounding a death. I learned that these reactions, which can last for days or weeks at a time, often give rise to a host of emotions and physical problems.

Adult grief is different. Anniversary reactions pummeled me into the ground. Not only was the grief of 9/11 unbearable by itself, but it catapulted me into the past, where all my tender spots surfaced at once, leaving me vulnerable and exposed.

It's not an accident that I can't remember why I bothered going to film school, or why I drink more red wine, or why I'm fed up with New York City, a city I was passionate about until the moment I wasn't. For a short period, I will not know what to do. For a short period, I will place my hopes in the sunny, frolic feeling of California and then learn that sunshine only makes the contrast more severe. For a short period, everything I know about myself will unravel like a small snag on a sweater. There will be no more hiding in my garage attic.

Some things will have to come to an end.

6.

where from here
a ribbon of land smoking
within the girl's hair smoking
there are bodies here
micro mosaic children
a triptych exile against wall
my dead are rescued
a closing of crossings
a scatter vapor of earth
a trance of metal
where from here
i am all tunnel

Suheir Hammad, *Zeitoun*

Did I dream about the sheet falling on my bed? No. The moment is excruciating, but there I am wishing for it to come back so I can feel something again. I have no experience with this. I've yet to grow up. A world without memory is a world of the present. At ten, I pray for only memories because the present is filled with loneliness. At fifteen, I pray that I won't forget what she sounded like. At twenty, I feel bad that I haven't thought of her often. At thirty, I pray to learn how to live in a world without memory. At forty, I give up trying to replace her.

Victoria loved to sleep. Virginia loved to wake up. There were lots of scary reasons for her to come to my room and ask to sleep with me. First, it was the spider and then the shadows and then the dark altogether, which I explained was never going to go away because nighttime happens every night. There was always enough reason to knock gently and ask to sleep with me as if she had never asked me before. "If Mom had wanted us to sleep together, she would have gotten us one bed," I'd say, and she would remain standing there, which was the ritual. Then I'd say yes as if it were the first time instead of the millionth time, and we would eat snow outside my window, look at the stars, or play the nose kissing game. The object of the game was to take turns kissing each other's noses until the kiss could barely be felt. The game is harder than it sounds when playing in the dark. Once we tried it with the tips of our tongues, but we abandoned it because it grossed us out.

According to Rabindranath Tagore, there is a sublime paradox that lies at the root of existence. "We never can go around it, because we never can stand outside the problem and weigh it against any other possible alternative." When I became an adult, I gave up on my suspicions about God because life itself had become too mysterious. If I had read Anne Carson when I was ten, I would have learned I cannot "get around the back of God." The death of my sister will simultaneously draw me towards "God," and away from all popular notions of who or what God is.

Saint Teresa of Ávila considered the life of prayer to be the greatest manifestation of the theological life of the faithful who, believing in the love of God, free themselves from everything to attain the full presence of that love [in the service of others]. In her seminal work, *The Interior Castle*, this prominent Spanish mystic, religious reformer, author, and theologian pictures her spiritual journey from outside of a crystal, global castle to the center room where the King lives and where the soul, the individual, is invited into a deep union.

Where is the center of myself, and how do I buy a ticket to get there?

To get to the center, one must travel through the "four waters." The first water is vocal prayer and discursive meditation; the second water is when the soul begins to recollect itself, bordering on the supernatural. The third stage, says St. Teresa, is a genuine union marked by "a sleep of the faculties." And finally, in the fourth water, St. Theresa describes her experience of union with God as a completely mystical partnership in this way:

> In this fourth water the soul isn't in possession of its senses, but it rejoices without understanding what it is rejoicing in. It understands that it is enjoying a good in which are gathered together all goods, but this good is incomprehensible. All the senses are occupied in this joy in such a way that none is free to be taken up with any other exterior or interior thing.

Basically, she was an avid meditator who could transcend thought, and in doing so attained access to her own divine nature. I found her quite enchanting. I also came to understand why people find God such an appealing concept in light of tragedy or grief, as there is no bigger blanket of comfort. There is no more powerful an idea than to believe in the overwhelming benevolence of a higher power that has a plan. And while my family will take comfort under this blanket, I will go in search of a new vocabulary.

Every religion in the world has a name for what it means to "try," as I call it. One "practices" Buddhism. In Taoism, one "walks" the way. In Christianity, one is "born again," and in Shamanism, one does "the work." It turns out, I'm a very hard worker.

7.

Walk around feeling like a leaf.
Know you could tumble any second.
Then decide what to do with your time.

Naomi Shihab Nye, *The Art of Disappearing*

My late thirties found me entirely preoccupied with time, in a fascinating Einstein kind of way. I would regularly fantasize about calling my sister up. You know, like she lived down the street from me, and we would get together for lunch and talk about her kids and her husband and about me not having kids yet and the joy of not having a husband and about shopping and food and friends and our parents. I would like to show her my stories, and we would kiss goodbye quickly as people do when they are sure they are going to see each other again. I would just like to call her up. And so, I did. I dreamt that I sat in my baby blue room explaining to the others that quantum physics has theoretically made this possible. There is no reason why I should not be able to call her up at the pajama party that she never attended because she died on the way. I dialed the eighteen-digit long-distance number. My heart froze; we got cut off. I dialed again, impatient. Rachel answered and laughed her laugh, calling for Gina to come to the phone. I could hear all the static, a party-line I thought, while all these international voices were saying wise and serendipitous things. I am not satisfied, so I wait. Finally, I hear her faint girlish voice—it is mellow and calm and joyful. It's hers, just as I remembered it, and then we got cut off again. "Hello, it's me," she says.

The Upanishads hold that the subtlest of the five senses is hearing. It is the first to awaken in the fetus and the last to leave the body at death, as the wisdom traditions recognized by reading sacred texts to the dying or recently dead. "Why is everyone saying the Hail Mary over and over again," I ask at the age of seven while sitting in my grandmother's living room. In the early seventies, my grandparents' (on my mother's side) living room was decorated in hues of brown and orange with accents of yellow. A tweed living room sofa set and delicate Mexican colonial wooden accent chairs. There was an old Victrola and large antique standing radio with a huge knob. In the corner was a bar with cabinets that my grandfather made by hand. The entire house smelled like vanilla and freshly prepared food. We kids could opt out of these rosary rituals, but for some reason, I found them fascinating. "So they can hear us helping them get to the other place," was my Tía Maggie's reply. This only prompted more questions until I was told to hush up or leave the room. If the deceased was of questionable character, the rosary would be interminably long.

I tried to put this particular part of the puzzle in some order. Certainly, being able to hear Gina's voice after twenty some odd years has to be significant; it has to be a major milestone in memory. There is some quantum relationship here, and my desire to feel the past, present and future happening simultaneously are so strong and poignant that the idea of not being able to access each one with clarity and a sense of knowing makes me very, very tired. Steve Hagen says, "Unlike animals, we fool ourselves about death. We think we know that we're going to die. But death isn't something we can know as an idea. What we call 'death' is only something we imagine." What difference does it make now? She's dead and her voice is just a sound that disappears when I wake up.

July 1975. My sister is standing behind me on the high dive because I've decided at the last minute that I'm terrified of jumping into the water. It's the last lesson of our summer swim class, and I'm about to be humiliated by my younger sister. I'm the one who begged my mother for swimming lessons. I'm the one who agreed we'd get our hair chopped off so as not to have to wear swim caps. I'm the one who was first in my class to make it to the floating deck. At this horrible moment, I'm stuck on the high dive and can't get my feet to move. Our mother works full-time, so our grandmother Emilia takes us to swim lessons at Carls' quarry. The Carls go to our church, and my mom is a good friend of Joanne and Dennis, who also own the campground nearby. The campground and quarry are two of my favorite places on earth. Our family would take up several large sites that connected via tiny trails. My mom would play the guitar, and we'd be allowed to walk around at night because everyone knew each other. It was mysterious. I loved watching people sitting around their campfires, and the smell of mosquito repellant and hot dogs was very comforting.

I climb the ladder with full intention to finally, after all this time, jump off the high dive, but when I get to the edge, I'm terrified to do it. I'm so surprised at myself. My grandmother, Emilia is watching from the grass.

I walk slowly to the edge of the diving board and stare at my water-logged toes. I curl them over the scratchy surface and look into the black shiny water. Lightly, lightly—the wind blows goosebumps on my skin. I walk back to where my sister is standing and, without words, she pushes me aside and walks to the edge of the diving board, pinches her nose, and jumps. She screams and then splashes; into the water, she goes. I hold my breath, waiting for her to come up, and when she does, I'm both relieved and embarrassed. I'm told by my swimming coach, the oldest of the Carl sisters, that I will have to jump or else she will come up and push me. I hate her. I used to want to be her because she was the lifeguard. She doesn't understand who I am. She doesn't understand that I'm the brave one; I'm a better swimmer than everyone in my class, and it was my big idea to take her swim classes in the first place—and I think that should count for something. But something has come over me. Not only does my sister jump before me, but she climbs right back up the ladder in her multicolored striped bathing suit, "Watch me. I'm going to do it again," and walks off the board for the second time. My life is over.

I'm told to jump. "I don't want to do it!" I scream down to my grandmother, hoping that she will say I don't have to jump if I don't want to. She responds, "Do it for Grandma!" If the phrase "fuck it" had been in my vocabulary, I would have called upon it. Instead, I turn and walk off the board, flying into the water where I immediately begin flapping my arms and legs as fast as I can, just as I was told to. I furiously bat my legs and arms; afraid I will run out of breath. I imagine a large fish-type animal lunging for my flippery feet and pulling me down into the dark water. But before I know it, I pop up to the surface triumphant and completely unrecognizable from the person I was before this achievement. I jump two more times, once more than my sister in order to regain my self-esteem and bring my world back to order.

On the way to the car, my grandmother says she's very proud of us. We both sit in the front seat of my grandmother's maroon Chevrolet Impala wrapped in our towels. I get the window because I'm the oldest. I look over at my sister and say those were good jumps. I liked yours more, she says.

8.

Easy actions of the mind not subject to reality. Among the
luxuries a safe life affords: imagining the worst.

Boyer Rickel, *"On Consciousness"*

May 19, 1978. It's nighttime when our parents arrive back at my
aunt's house. I'm told my mom is waiting for me outside. Years later,
I'll think this was probably my mother's idea—to give me some
privacy. She tells me there's been a terrible accident. "I'll go get my
shoes," is the first thing I say. I won't be going anywhere. I'm told
that my sister is in heaven. Heaven? I stare at my feet and the first
thought that comes to my mind is that Gina is good at walking on the
rocks in her bare feet, but I've always needed shoes. The driveway
rocks, my feet, the car I lean on, stuck like glue. I've made a terrible
mistake. I could've saved her because I was older, stronger, faster,
and more powerful. I was her protector; it was my job and I failed.

I didn't get to go to the hospital. I didn't get to see her dead, which
only adds to the illusion that it never really happened. I didn't get to

decide what to do with her clothes or her things. Where did they go and who has them? Why didn't I think to keep something? I didn't get to decide what she wore to her funeral, even though I'm the one who knew what her favorite outfit was. I didn't get to decide what music we would listen to or what prayers we would recite, even though I knew what songs and prayers she loved most, from catechism class. I didn't get to decide when I went back to school, which would've been never.

Going to school was like having a disease. The teachers were comforting, most students stayed away. What do you say? "Sorry your sister is dead; do you want to play kickball?" I didn't get to decide anything. It took twenty years for me to realize that it was my mother who had to make all those decisions by herself, and the fact that I was not old enough to help her made me very sad.

Memoria of Maria Teresa Garza

I remember that as soon as each of you girls was born, your dad and I would call Ama Lolita, your great-grandmother on my side. The first thing she'd say is, "On your way home from the hospital, stop at church and offer the child to God. It is God's child and on loan to you." I believed her. But when Gina died, I was challenged because I now had to live what I always professed to believe. How was I going to do it?

Your father had moved out of the house in November 1977. In April, he moved back to Texas. You girls were very sad. He wrote a letter that he wanted me to read to you after his departure, but I decided to hang onto it until a more appropriate time.

I had been invited to be part of the team for a non-denominational retreat weekend, the last weekend in April, and I accepted. I became aware early in the weekend that God was speaking to me. Through various people, he was saying: "Trust me, don't be afraid, no matter what, I am with you." It seemed strange to me at the time how often this message was repeated throughout the weekend. When you are part of a spiritual retreat like that, your senses are heightened and if you are open, you can receive a lot of guidance. At the end, on Sunday afternoon, during the walkthrough (where family members of the people who participated in the retreat get to see each other), Gina was the first through the line and ran up to hug me. It had seemed as though Gina had been there with me, throughout the weekend, and that God had been speaking to her also. She told me about the thoughts she'd been having while I was away, and I felt this tremendous closeness to her. Although both of you often attended these types of gatherings with me, it was your sister who really enjoyed them.

When we got home on Sunday night, I shared with the both of you that your dad had left for Texas, but that he had left a letter for you. I read the letter while you both sat on the stairs. Afterward, Gina said she would never see your dad again. Of course, I thought she was just missing him so I tried to reassure the both of you that we could easily go visit during summer break and the holidays. However, Gina quietly insisted that she would never see her dad again and nothing I said seemed to reassure her. Of course, she was right. She never did see him again.

During the next few weeks, things were not quite right, but I really couldn't pinpoint what had changed. On the 16th or 17th of May, Gina had eaten a whole quart of strawberries that I had set aside for a strawberry shortcake dessert I was making for a meeting at the church. I was so busy. I got home from work and expected to be able to just make this dessert really quick, but the strawberries were gone, and it wouldn't be easy for me to get some more. She was deeply sorry for what she'd done, saying she knew she shouldn't be eating the whole quart of strawberries but that somehow, she just couldn't help herself. Later that evening, she wrote me a note saying how sorry she was about doing that, she had asked God to forgive her, and He had, so she hoped that I would too. I still have that note.

It was May 19th, 1978. You girls were waiting anxiously for this day to come around because you were attending your cousin Rachel's pajama party. I wouldn't be home until late that day and so I asked your Tío Manuel [Tía Maggie's husband] to take you to your Tía Eva's for the party. He picked both of you up and headed back to his house, then onto your Tía Eva's.

In the meantime, I left work and stopped at Tony Packo's for dinner since I was going to cut grass upon arriving home. At some point, I became aware of a very uncomfortable sensation, and I attributed it to missing you both tremendously, wishing I'd been able to see you before you left. I just really wanted to be with you. I knew that rushing home wasn't going to solve that since you had already been picked up and were on your way to your Tía Eva's.

I arrived home, changed clothes, and started mowing the lawn. When I got done, I drove to Jack's Superette for a six-pack of beer. When I returned, my friend Pat told me that your grandmother had called and to call her back. I called Mom and she told me that there had been an accident and that Dad had told her to just wait there until they heard from him again. As far as I knew, both of you were in the vehicle, and the last thing I was going to do was wait at home for news. I told Mom I was going to the hospital, so she asked that I pick her up. I was thirty-two years old and had never smoked in front of your grandmother, but on the way to the hospital that day, I lit up a cigarette in front of her. I had no idea what to expect. I did not expect the worst. Dad had told Mom that Connie was in critical condition, but no one said anything about you and Gina.

Upon my arrival at the hospital, no one would say anything until I was directed to a family room alongside the emergency area where I found many of my brothers and sisters. It was then that I was told that Gina and Connie had died. It was then that I was informed that you had stayed behind, that you had decided at the last minute to get out of the truck. Father Shanahan (who had been our pastor at Our Lady of

Mt. Carmel) was the chaplain on duty. He took me back to see my little girl. I cannot describe the sadness. I cannot do it. Something happened in me. I was looking at my baby and couldn't help but see Our Blessed Virgin de Guadalupe. And I thought if our blessed mother had to go through the agony of witnessing her son's death then I could go through the agony of witnessing my daughter's. For some reason, this was a great source of strength for me. I was also reminded of my grandmother's saying, "Our kids are not our own, but are on loan to us." Those two thoughts carried me. I knew there was something else, outside and inside of me, because after seeing Gina, I had to call your dad and his family, and then I had to tell you and I honestly don't know how I did it.

I cannot describe how hard it was for me to tell you that your little sister and cousin had died. I knew that I wouldn't have any good answers for you, and you were a person who would want them. I don't really remember what I said, but I did the best I could, I think. You kept saying that you should have been in the truck. I kept telling you that it was not meant to be. I tried to explain that God had a plan for the girls and other plans for you. I went through a lot during the time of the funeral because I had to make so many arrangements, and the decision as to whether to show the body or not was very difficult. I had the added stress of having to host your father and his parents. I thought of you. I knew you would want to see Gina, but I didn't want you to remember your sister other than how she was when she was alive. She was so beautiful. I decided on a closed casket.

My sister shakes her head in her way, to get the hair out of her face, and smiles at me from the truck I just climbed out of. I imagine my mom and me standing there watching her from the yard. I'm so sad, I say. My mother holds out her cupped hands. Give your sadness to me, she says, I'll hold it for you.

9.

We should take care not to make the intellect our god;
it has, of course, powerful muscles but no personality.
It cannot lead; it can only serve.

Albert Einstein

I'm eight and she's seven. I check up on her regularly. When I finally
find my sister, she is trapped underneath the kiddy slide. There is the
blacktop playground for the big kids and the kiddy playground for the
little ones. There is a boy who won't let her out, and his teasing has
both a flirtatious and mean tone to it. When I ask what he's doing, he
laughs too loudly and still won't let her out. I grab him by the collar
and pull him out from under the kiddy slide and swing him so hard he
flies backward and falls to the ground. My sister jumps from under the
slide and follows me as I proceed to beat up her classmate. I pin him
on the ground and hurt him until his laughs become tears and the
playground monitor is called to rescue him. My sister is peeking
through the small window into the gymnasium from the blacktop
playground, smiling at me and sticking out her tongue. She should

act more grateful. I'm in detention for a week. My only regret is that I apologized to him, an unavoidable compromise to lessen my sentence. A week later my parents tell us they are getting divorced.

No tears, just plain old common sense. Our parents are getting separated, which I already knew to be a euphemism for divorce. I know then that my parents are not right for each other, even though they are both right for us. We're called over from my great-aunt Lupe's house next door into a town hall meeting in our living room because my mother wants to do everything the right way. We enter the sacred circle of adults, our parents, our grandparents, a few aunts and uncles, and of course, Father Tony Gallagher, our Irish priest. We (I can say "we" because I'm the oldest) feel justifiably important; our opinions matter and our advice is often sought out in family matters.

"Your father and I have decided to get separated, and we want you to know that we both love you two very much and it's not your fault." Divorce had just started to get fashionable. Jodi Wilson's parents are divorced, I thought to myself. "How do you feel? Would you like to say something?" "May we be excused, please? We have to go to the bathroom," I say, grabbing my sister's hand. Off we go to the bathroom. I lock the door behind us. We don't do anything at first, and then I proceed to open the drawer and then the vanity. I put my elbows on the counter and my hands on both sides of my cheeks, like when I watch TV. I turn the faucet on and then off. My sister can't reach the counter, so I pick her up and we look at each other in the mirror, then I put her back down. "Well, I guess we should go back." "Yeah," she says softly. "Do you want to cry or something?" "No," she says." "Me neither." So back we go and there we sit. All the faces look big and cautious and sad. We hug our dad, then our mom. My

~ 45 ~

dad looks a little broken, but I know my mom will be fine because she is strong. "Sorry you have to get a divorce," I say. "Yeah, sorry we have to get a divorce," says my sister. We told them not to feel bad and then asked if we could go watch *The Six Million Dollar Man.*

Gina and I always had vivid imaginations. The sky in our world was more than blue; it was silky and watery and slippery. We could fly in it and swim in it at the same time. Gina flies, I swim. Off we go flying and swimming, but I'm the leader and she's my assistant and we speak telepathically. Gina is an expert at decoding non-verbal communication. She saves me from my brooding self.

"You want to talk?"

"No," I say.

"Why are you so cranky?"

"I'm not!"

"That's true. You are the happiest person I know," she says.

"That's not what you're supposed to say," I say.

"Why?"

"You're supposed to say, Yes, you are, then I say, no I'm not, and then we have an argument and I win."

"Win what?"

"The argument."

"What for?"

"So that someone can win. That's why people have arguments so that someone can be the winner."

"What does the winner win?"

"The argument."

"I want to win a car," she says.

"You can't win a car; you don't even drive, and you're only six years old."

"You're seven."

"I know I'm seven, and I can't get my permit till I'm sixteen."

"When will I get my permit?"

"When you're sixteen, the same as me, but I get to drive first."

"When will I be sixteen?"

"You're six now, so six + what equals sixteen?"

"I hate math."

"So do I, but use your fingers, this one's easy."

"Ten."

"And for me it's nine 'cause I'm older."

"But you don't have a car."

"Dad will get me one."

"Did he say?"

"Uh-huh."

"He didn't tell me he'd get me one."

"That's because you will get my car, and then I will get a new one."

"I want a new one."

"You can't have a new one if you're just learning to drive; you'll have
to take mine."

"I want a pink one."

"It won't be pink."

"Why?"

"Because pink is gross."

"I want it to be yellow."

"It won't be yellow either. You have to take the color you get; it will
probably be blue."

"But blue is your favorite color," she says.

"I know, but there are millions of blue cars everywhere. They don't
make pink cars."

"But blue is your favorite color, not mine."

"Change it."

"Change what?"

"Your favorite color. Blue is everywhere, the sky is half the world and it's blue, and the oceans are more than half the world and they're all blue..."

"Not the lakes."

"No, those are dirty."

"Lake Erie is like a blue, brown, green color."

"Yeah, but most water and skies are blue so everywhere I look is my favorite color. You can change yours if you want."

"Mine is yellow."

"There's not much that's yellow."

"Uh-huh. The sun is yellow and every day it lights up the whole world and your blue sky and your blue oceans, and if it didn't, everything would die and turn black, and black is no one's favorite color."

"That's true," I say, "I never thought of it that way."

When we were four- and five years old, I remember staying at my great-grandmother Ama Lolita's house. We wanted to sleep in her room with her because it was a mystical magical Mexican room filled with fresh flowers, candles, an altar, and it smelled both wild and sweet, like juniper, cinnamon, and vanilla. It's barely dawn, and I awaken softly to see my great-grandmother reciting the rosary in front of her bedroom altar, as she has done her whole life. Two small white novella candles are glowing, casting her in silhouette. I see her shadow rocking back and forth and her rosary beads hanging from her small hands. At first, I am afraid. But then I quickly understand, even as a child, that she is in a reverie, and I should take care not to make any sounds that might distract her. I listen to her whispered prayers in Spanish, repeated with a cadence and rhythm that is distinctly her own. What has always been peculiar to me about this memory is that I don't recall what my feelings about it were. I listened and watched her for several nights during that stay without any realization in my mind that I was enjoying it so much. I wanted very much for my sister to wake up and watch Ama Lolita praying. But the one time I tried to nudge her awake, she started giggling in her sleep, so I stopped and kept the experience to myself. Prayer or meditation, chanting or mantra, ceremony or ritual. Bliss is achievable in a small Texas room at dawn.

10.

I have a leaping impulse, an arrow
of wheat, and a bow at my breast clearly waits,
and a thin throb, of water and tenacity,
like something that perpetually breaks,
pierces my separations to the depths,
extinguishes my power and spreads my grief.

Pablo Neruda, "Daily Mourner"

August 2000. Jane tells me about meeting Don Juan in her Grecian apartment by the sea. Fantasy, energy fields, infinite possibilities in the infinite world; molecular re-organization while we float naked. I want a supernatural visit, too. Instead, Kim pours me another glass of Champagne—it'll have to do, and it always does. It's the summer I fall in love with Champagne, the summer I realize that you don't need a special occasion to drink it, the summer Kim teaches me the joy of cooking for people you love, the summer I realize that I should focus on the movement of the psyche toward what seems good to it at the moment—a movement of spirit, Dante calls it. Jane and Kim live on

Acacia Lane, and this is the summer of beautiful moments. I decide to no longer swallow my melancholy. I won't do that anymore. I've changed. Linda, the desert therapist I could afford to see only twice, tells me I can use another toolkit. So, I hammer my head, saw off my ears, nail my heart, put my new tools into my new tool belt and walk down the street, feeling like only parts of a person. I could tear myself into pieces, and gather the bits that serve me, like stage direction.

During this period, Pablo Neruda's *Residence on Earth* is a bedside staple. The bilingual collection of poems is enough to excite C every evening as she recites out loud the Spanish side of his poems and waits for my critique of her pronunciation. If she's way off, she insists I correct her in that very moment, but I learn quickly that if I do as she insists, she will start the poem over from the very beginning. It doesn't matter really; she'll start it over anyway, or she'll read it several times until she sounds to herself like she knows how to speak Spanish.

Reading poetry is like medicine. In fact, I begin to realize that all things that calmly stamp the heart are medicine. Neruda proves this theory, and I neatly pack the information into a vault that's labeled: The Things Understood. And what will become the greatest shock and my most bewildering lesson (and only later will feel so ridiculously obvious) is that the someone who can so lovingly caress that part of your soul that helps you breathe, can also stomp and choke it. C makes a promise...

> in your madness and your mystery
> you reveal yourself to me
> it is safe, we cannot walk upon such space
> we shall not tread on this

it is sacred and strange
I will guard you from the world
I will not let
the others walk upon you
or let another into
this sanctuary of you

Rosemarie Waldrop asks, "Is it possible to locate the ledge of your promises to lean my head on?" I decide, no, it is not safe to believe a poem scrawled on a paper napkin. I've come to understand that it's hard to assess the beginning or the end of a relationship, but you always know when you are nearing the beginning of the end.

At the beginning of our friendship, C came to my Park Slope, Brooklyn brownstone after working her shift at the World Trade Center, and I served her red wine in a small juice glass. Luxurious. It was late afternoon, and she'd brought over a book, *Evidence*, by Luc Sante. It was a photo-essay book on death portraits, which also had old photos of crime scenes and victims found in a forgotten storage room when Grand Central was being renovated. How odd, I thought at the time, that she was reading a book this horrible and beautiful.

We were talking about details that people remember about tragedies, I think. I said in a deadpan way, "Oh, that's funny, I just remembered the gravel hurting my feet on the driveway when I found out my sister was dead. The gravel never hurt her feet." Up until then, I had never mentioned my sister, but perhaps I trusted this person who was reading about dead strangers. Surely, this person will understand me, protect me, and help me put away my seriousness.

But no, instead the relationship will be a resting spot for my sorrow.

Four years later, it's a calm, still night, and we are still at the beginning of the end. My head is on fire, melting from the inside and pouring out my nose, leaving residual coals in my throat. I wake up drenched in the wee hours wondering why C always picks the worst times to make an irrelevant point. What point? I have no idea. She's mad at everything and finally feels safe enough to express herself. There are boundaries made of chalk everywhere. Memory is called into question. Like an act that erases all that's come before—like falling in love—but the opposite.

We had already decided that an impossible conversation, a kind of non-conversation, can happen only to those who speak the same language, a sort of code. I only knew something about love after having fallen into it. Like falling down a flight of stairs, it is over by the time I reach the bottom and now I'm standing up, trying to make it look like I'm not broken or embarrassed. I quickly pull my shirt over my head and smile in a room full of people drinking wine and chatting about politics, books, or the latest film. I am humbled in the face of how little I understand about love, and yet my heart feels too big for my body. I put this too, in my "Things Understood" vault.

Old habits, old ideas, and old thoughts are unraveling, as they should, but I'm not prepared. Film school is over and the last thing I want to do is make a fucking movie. My relationship is falling apart, slow piece by slow piece. I've decided to pull out these tightly woven threads on a sweater I've worn my whole life, the sweater that makes me feel safe and guarded, and cautious. The love I thought I always had for myself is called into question by the mere fact that I can't seem to get what I want from someone else.

11.

Clouds come floating into my life, no longer to carry rain or usher storm, but to add color to my sunset sky.

Rabindranath Tagore, *Sadhana*

March 2008. Alice, Texas. A week after my grandfather's death my dad and my great aunt Tía Eloisa pick me up at the airport. On the way home, I hear my dad's story of his father's death. I enter the mortuary and walk up to my grandmother, who sits in her wheelchair close to the casket. She weeps at the sight of me. I hold her fleshy arms as she squishes my face into her shoulder. She won't let go so I stand there, half kneeling, half standing, holding her. She weeps out loud during the slideshow when they are projecting photos of my grandfather. I have to relax, I tell myself. This is going to be a process.

After the viewing, I share the car with my dad's sister Tía Julie and her husband Tío Roy, who is wearing black jeans, cowboy boots, and a black leather blazer. He wears a gold medallion of La Virgen de Guadalupe around his neck. He's always cared about the way he looks. My Tía Julie has a master's degree in education, but she could be a standup comic. We all go to Whataburger and my uncle says he has to have his bun toasted. "I want mine toasted too," I say, even though I have no intention of eating fast food. Tía Eloisa says, "I'll take mine semi-toasted." And Tía Julie jokes, "Hay mira, I want my bun toasted on the top, and normal on the bottom." Laughter ensues while everyone tries to come up with a million ways to order their buns toasted until the quips turn into other jokes. The saying "beating a dead horse" does not come close to my family's knack for trying to outdo each other in the funny department. I'm tired and rest my head on my Tía Eloisa's shoulder. She puts her hand on my face, "Calientita la cara de la bebita," (the baby's face is hot) and keeps it there, patting me every so often while beating the horse with my Tía Julie. Two years from this moment, my Tía Eloisa will die of cancer in her early seventies and two years after that my Tío Roy will die of lung cancer. I will have the memory of my aunt's hand on my face to send me back to the backseat of my Tío Roy's car, his sweet voice, the smell of department store perfume, the pungent Texas nighttime, and a car full of Spanish laughter.

My grandmother is in bed when we arrive home and must remind me, as I slip into my pajamas, that she and grandpa haven't spent a day apart in sixty-five years. She touches my leg.

Old people in my family need to touch the younger people. "He loved me," she says in Spanish. When they were first married, they lived with my great grandmother, Ama Tola, because my grandfather didn't want to screw up his marriage, and knew that with his mother's help, he'd stay in line. They lived there for twelve years. My father comes in to say goodnight and sits on the edge of his mother's twin bed and soothingly caresses her arm, listening to her recite the past.

When my father was a young child, he fell very ill. My grandmother was so worried he wouldn't survive that she gave him over to Ama Tola. After my father's health was restored, Ama Tola announced that my father would live with her from then on. Since my father's parents only lived down the street, there was agreement. My father was known around the neighborhood as Azucarau, "the sweetened." No one dared touch him.

It was a tiny canary-yellow house that sat on large bricks. Chickens everywhere, a garden in the back and an outhouse. My great-grandfather Tomás, although they had indoor plumbing, refused to shit in the house where he ate and slept. He had a casita, which was just large enough for a full bed, a large washbasin, and an outhouse in the back of the dirt yard. During his siesta, we would throw stones on the roof, which was made of Mexican tin. The stones would clink and clatter and cascade down to the dirt. For some reason, this made us happy. Since Apa Tomás slept in his casita, my father grew up sleeping with his grandmother. After he was bathed, fed, and sporting clean underwear, he would crawl into bed. With her back to him, my father would hold his hands in prayer and tuck them in between my grandmother's side and the mattress. And even years later as a grown man, visiting, he would crawl in bed behind his grandmother and tuck his hands in prayer and fall asleep. He still sleeps with his hands tucked in prayer.

Memoria of Jesse Garza

I was in Texas by then and it was another routine day, no different from the day before. I was in my favorite bar doing what I did best at that time, drinking. My brother-in-law walked in and made his way over to my table and told me I needed to go home, that it was very important. My grandmother was in the local hospital and had been there for some time, so I asked my brother-in-law if Ama Tola had died. He wouldn't answer me. It made me mad, but he was so agitated and hurrying to get home, so I stopped asking him questions. I felt sure it was about Ama and knew that she was going to pass away soon so even though I felt a great sense of loss, I thought I could bear it. My love for her was great because she had raised me since I was a baby. How to say it? The weight of my world just crumbled down on top of me when I was told your sister was killed in a car accident. The pain can't possibly be any less than having my heart torn out of my chest. I couldn't breathe. I couldn't speak. I would lay down my life for my girls and there I was, hopeless and empty, and useless. When I had calmed down enough, they told me Connie died as well.

Friends and relatives made the arrangements for the trip back to Ohio. One friend, Elva, furnished her car. She was a special friend and knew me so well that all she had to do was be there for me. She didn't talk to me or hold me, and I really appreciated that. Every thought I had was centered on the pain of it all, "What am I going to do?" I need my Gina. I talked only when I had to. So many things were going through my mind, confusing me. I silently talked to God a lot. Everyone likes to use the expression "God's will," but I think that's bullshit. God doesn't kill, people do. I know that now, but at the time of Gina's death, I only blamed God. The trip seemed to take forever.

There were moments of comfort. Those brief moments would come when I thought of you. I would switch my thoughts to you being alive and that would give my heart a needed break.

But the hurt was so great that it began to overwhelm me. That's when my sister stopped in a town somewhere to find me a doctor. She explained the situation, and I was given a prescription for Valium. It worked! I fell asleep immediately and slept for most of the remainder of the trip. When we finally arrived in Ohio, your mom and I consoled each other for a moment, but mostly I dwelled on the loss. No one could comfort me. The only time I felt any relief was when you got near me. In you, I felt as though Gina was still alive. It's hard to describe what I mean by that, but it was such a relieving sensation. The day of the funeral was the saddest most painful day of my life. My baby girl was going to be put in the ground forever. Never again would I see her smile or hear her giggle. I wanted so badly to take her place. I had made a real mess of my life and the only thing good about it were you girls, and now one of you was gone.

I was still a mess actually, barely coping, and I knew that my grief would have no end, and I was right. I came to accept her death, but the grief is eternal. It never goes away. Gina is more than memory. She took a part of me with her. But I really believe that she left you her share of life. It's as if you are doubly powerful, as if Gina breathed into you her entire self, I can't really explain it.

When I got back to Texas, I suppose I thought that I was going to heal. Thing is, healing never happens, not really. That is just a load of crap people say when they don't know what to say. You just become different. Ama Tola died about a month later, never knowing about Gina's death, so I thought. I mean, we kept it from her but towards the end of her life, she started mentioning a little girl by her bed. I got goosebumps when I realized she was talking to Gina. The reason I know is that she had an expression that only she used to describe Gina's hair. I felt so strange but so relieved.

My life is tranquil now. I quit drinking thirty years ago, and my health has deteriorated some, but for the most part, I'm doing good. I have lived a pretty good life. What wasn't good was entirely my fault. I'm convinced that life is what we make it towards the later years. I count and sort out the memories, sort of re-live them in my mind, just in case I kick the bucket suddenly. I will leave this world knowing that you are strong and that you'll always be fine, and Gina lives on in you. I will die happy knowing that I helped bring into this world two unbelievable girls. My girls. I will die happy knowing that.

In March of 2013, my dad and I coast down Texas Route 281, listening to Rocio Durcal, one of his favorite Spanish artists. I ask him what Ama Tola's (my great-grandmother) name really was, having never thought to ask until now. Teodala, he says, is a very unusual name, even back then. I say, Theodora? I had no idea my great grandmother's name was Theodora, or that my grandmother's name, which was Ama Mela is really short for Manuela, or that my grandfather's name, Apa Chele, is really short for Marcelino. You can live a whole life and only know one single slice of a person. Who was Teodala, the old woman in the canary yellow house, before she became my Ama Tola?

12.

The Soul is tied to no individual, no culture, no tradition, but rises fresh in every person, beyond every person, and grounds itself in a truth and glory that bows to nothing in the world of time and place and history.

Ken Wilber, *The Essential Ken Wilber*

Four months after my sister died, I'm in the yard throwing a softball high into the air and maneuvering to catch it—I hear myself saying, "You can't get completely under it, stupid—you have to place yourself just right or an easy catch will get all messed up." I am speaking to no one in particular. I throw the ball so high in fact that I have time to notice that she's not there. Not today, not tomorrow, not ever. So, I play a game. I throw the ball really high and when I catch it, and I always do because that's how good I am, she'll be sitting there eating an orange. So, I throw, then catch, then look. Nowhere. I didn't throw it high enough, so I throw again, then catch, then look. I have to stop immediately; I've ruined it altogether. I decide to run myself ragged all over the yard. I run in circles, then I run laps, and then I run sideways until I collapse. But she's still not there. When I drag myself inside the house sweaty and out of breath, I find my mother crying softly on the sofa. I panic. What do I say? Her legs are crossed, and she looks so young sitting there, her hand over her eyes, trying to compose herself now that she's noticed I'm there. I'm not my sister. I'm the athletic, talkative, opinionated one. I'm the one who wakes up cranky, can't sit still, and talks too much. I'm not the one who loves church, prays out loud, and apologizes when I mess up. I'm not the one who can comfort my mother when she is feeling overwhelmed with her life and grieving for her baby girl. I recognize the situation because it happens to me. I'll just be sitting around and bam! I get slammed with "that sudden" feeling. I see clearly in this moment that my mother has it. I sit down next to her and place my sweaty hand on her arm. But I have no words.

In August of 2002, I move to Los Angeles and live with my friend Michelle and her six-year-old son, Weston, for six months (it was supposed to be three weeks) before renting a one-bedroom apartment in the same neighborhood of Echo Park. I'm still going through a slow breakup with C, as if riding a rollercoaster in slow motion. But Michelle takes people in. She listens to me, speaks softly, and harbors no judgments. Every time I explain to her my surprise regarding the turn of events, she will be surprised with me, not at me. Michelle, her partner Sage and her son Weston will come over and eat dinner with me, they will fill my house when it feels empty, and they will remind me that I'm fine. Weston and I will make nature documentaries called, for instance, "The Echo Park Lake Ducks." We will go to the Salton Sea and make a documentary about the migration of geese called the "Salton Sea Migration of Geese." In the first shot, which is Weston's idea, he runs into a long broad field that looks like it's covered in snow, but in reality, the white-colored fields are covered in geese. He stumbles out into the field as fast as he can go, and the geese soar up all at once. He likes this shot very much. We will go and watch Sage's band, The Lucky Stars, watch movies, and eat good food. They will guard me against too much time alone. They were the non-lonely moments of my loneliness.

I saw myself going through the motions of life, but more like a curious creature wondering how the movie was going to end. Loneliness looked like this: after Bella, the community cat, makes herself comfortable in her spot near the door, I make myself comfortable in mine and flip through identical television stations until landing on *The L Word*, a Showtime original series. I missed the first two seasons, and the current season is over, and I ponder that there is no way that Bette would've taken the baby; how ridiculous or typical that Shane left Carmen at the altar, or when is it that they will let Alice do something exciting because she's such a peculiar character. I should watch more television, I think to myself before I turn it off and return to the latest issue of *The New Yorker*, which I subscribed to because I wanted to feel like I knew what was going on in the literary and cultural landscape that was not my life. But first I need to make myself some tea, peppermint. By the time I make it back to my spot, because I get distracted walking through the dining room where I notice that I need to deal with my taxes, the teapot whistles, and I go back to the kitchen and make a snack to go with my tea.

I wipe a small spot of water off the counter.

The tea helps me relax, which no longer puts me in the mood to care about literature or culture, so I turn the television back on and catch the tail end of the current telenovela. I watch a beautiful woman cry real tears as her cold-hearted nemesis takes away her baby. The woman's arms are outstretched, pleading for her right to be a mother. Meanwhile, a man interrupts a couple dining at a fancy restaurant, accusing the woman that he will not let her get away with this. It's just like *The L Word*. Right now, I understand what is happening to me. I'm watching myself float through an evening where nothing makes me happy and yet nothing makes me sad. I am a witness to my own loneliness, which in turn dissolves the feeling somewhat. My life is not going to be good one day. It's good right now. I focus my attention on the distance I've placed between my situation and my feelings about it. I'm free. As my attention returns to the telenovela, I realize my family is tuned in to the same program and that thought comforts me. I think to myself that my grandfather Gilbrando would be quite proud of the fact that I have learned, in my adult years, how to be quiet. I am wrapping myself up or unraveling. Either way, I am not the same version of myself.

"Like a mummy," says my grandmother Emilia, who has wrapped me tightly in a large towel, so I can't move my arms. She lifts me out of the tub and transports me to the TV room and plops me next to my sister (who has already had her bath) to watch *Little House on the Prairie* where we eat Jiffy Pop popcorn with butter. My grandfather looks at me in his way, feigning distraction, and puts his finger to his lips in case I had any compulsion to begin talking. He makes the same gesture when he lets me go fishing with him. He says I talk too much and that's why we don't catch any fish. I try. I sit there and stare at the water in Metzger's Marsh and realize I can be really quiet when I want to be. I have a mouth full of popcorn and wink at him, and he can't help but laugh at me.

I dream my father and I are rowing a boat into Lake Erie. There's been a horrible flood. Everything has been lost. I sit at the tip of the boat and look back at my father, who is tirelessly rowing. I am ashamed to be alive. I am ashamed of not having saved my sister's life. My father rows farther out into the Great Lake. When it starts to rain, he lifts his head and opens his mouth to catch it. He smiles at me. I smile back and lift my head to catch raindrops on my tongue.

13.

Accept whatever comes to you woven in the pattern of your destiny, for what could more aptly fit your needs?

Marcus Aurelius

Where are we? I ask Gina.

We are in this room, she says.

Where is the room?

In our house.

Where is our house?

In this town.

Where is this town?

In this state.

Where is this state?

In this country.

Where is the country

On this planet.

Where is this planet?

In the solar system.

Where is the solar system?

In the galaxy.

Where is that?

In the universe.

Where is that?

Everywhere.

What is next door to the universe?

Everything.

What is on the other side of the universe?

Everyone.

The astonishing fact is that we don't know where we are. I'm in "Ecstasy: In and About Altered States" at MOCA in Los Angeles, standing in "Your strange certainty still kept (1996)." I'm frozen among the droplets that seem to be suspended in mid-air. An illusion created by a simple strobe light and a mist of water. Eliasson's installation makes me feel at home and I'm reminded that "Whether it is separated into drops or not, water is water. Our life and death are the same things." So says the Zen Buddhist Shunryu Suzuki. I'm lulled into a perception of arrested time and immediately conjure up a thought that eradicates any possibility of non-thought.

In a review of Mitchell's " *What Do Pictures Want? The Lives and Loves of Images,*" Ken Johnson says that it may not seem strange to say that a painting of an isolated house by Edward Hopper expresses sadness and loneliness, but it would be weird to claim that the painting itself is sad and lonely, somehow longing to be consoled or befriended. In the moment among the droplets of water, I was the one being consoled by the installation, and it reinforced quite profoundly my love of visual art, particularly the mixing of mediums. I don't know when my love of art started or if I had always had a fascination with it or if it was something that struck me after my sister's death, a way for me to be full of feeling and alone at the same time. Eventually, I found writing. I wrote short stories that were very short, like:

The Cup

When she had learned about art, her first painting was a Mexican cup because the cup was her grandmother's. And she loved her grandmother. She placed the cup near the window so it would cast shadows. When she finished, she looked at the cup but the love she felt for her grandmother was not there. It was the first and the last painting she ever painted.

While mingling inside the installation at MOCA, I imagined my mother hanging out with her cousin Miguel (a painter) and discussing activities that would be good for me after my sister died. Perhaps she heard me say something in passing or saw me flipping through elaborate picture books, because one day, just like that, Miguel was taking me to museums and teaching me how to draw. I loved the art supply store, and the aesthetics of all the colored paints, tubes, brushes, papers, and canvasses. Miguel started me out with oddly shaped pencils and then moved me to black and white charcoals, and then colored charcoals. I dropped painting because I think I loved it too much and was secretly terrified I'd be horrible at it. Instead, I became a filmmaker.

September 11, 2001, Corpus Christie, Texas. C and I are in the minivan with my Tía Eva and Tío Ernesto heading to Padre Island National Park when we get the news. "Someone is flying planes into the buildings in New York," says my dad. "You're lying," I say. This is my first response to catastrophic news of any kind. Why do I accuse the person delivering the news of being a liar? Your sister is in heaven. You're lying. We ask my uncle to turn on the radio while we pull into the Sears parking lot because my aunt needs to exchange a gift for her grandson. I stay in the van, staring out the window in complete silence. Suddenly an indescribable sadness mixed with apathy or maybe it's despair. Life feels dull and meaningless, and I have a moment of profound realization that most of my waking thoughts are not that important. How much energy do I waste thinking ridiculous thoughts? While sitting in an empty Sears parking lot in Corpus Christi, the world has taken on a surreal and confusing haze. I can smell the Gulf of Mexico, the birds mixed with that pungent Texas humidity smell that I love, and my heart feels like it's about to implode.

We debate on whether to cancel the beach and turn around and go home. The decision is made not to. I don't want to sit in front of a television set watching the horror—I know I won't miss anything that won't be shown again and again and again. I call my grandmother and ask her to make sure the family knows I'm not in New York. My mother's been fielding phone calls from family asking if I'm okay. I regularly worked five blocks from the World Trade Center. I try to call my New York friends, but the phones are dead. My friend Maryam Hassimi should be at work right this minute. But she's not. She, along with many others in the financial district, is being evacuated and running through the cavernous lower Manhattan streets to take cover inside churches and stores. After some time passes, she'll admit that she's been seeing a therapist for post-traumatic stress disorder. That same tragic day, one of my dearest friends, Amanda, presses her face into the grass at a nearby park to shield herself from the smoke and ash. I call Debra, a friend who is temporarily subletting our apartment in Park Slope, Brooklyn to tell her I hope this has not affected anyone she knows. She calls back to say her brother died in the South Tower.

My Tía Eva holds my hand as we all sit there looking out at the Gulf of Mexico as the waves roll in. We are numb, and in the same country, a thousand miles away, the city I live in is engulfed in ash. My disorganized feelings turn into an increasingly energetic and unstable formation. I imagine myself on a lifeboat in the middle of the Gulf of Mexico with a recognizable feeling of emptiness, a feeling I haven't visited in a very long time.

Back in New York, I take the train to Rockville Center, Long Island, and experience along with hundreds, a town that has suffered astonishing loss—an overwhelming number of people from Rockville died in the towers--the ritual for the people left behind.

Debra's brother is called Johnny. By all accounts, he was joyful and handsome. I know this only through pictures. I want her to share her grief with me, to tell me who he is, a man I've never met. This is the way of grief, I think. My heart flips vertically over its front end several times and into the ocean.

Long Beach and Johnny's Bench.

It's a strange coincidence. Debra is showing me the bench her family dedicated to Johnny right in front of a playground where Johnny's widow happens to be playing with her two sons. It's not far from where they grew up. Missy doesn't know me. She doesn't know I attended John's memorial service. She doesn't know that I know she was in Scotland visiting the cousin who is now standing beside me. She doesn't know that I know she spoke to John on the phone when the North Tower was hit and that he thought everything was going to be fine, or that I know he worked on the eighty something floor of the Second Tower. Or that I know her pain creeps up on her at any given moment. Or that I know she wonders what to say to her small boys, who wonder where their dad is.

She weeps while laughing—recounting, imitating what he'd say in his Long Island accent when asked what meal he'd prefer at a wedding he would never attend, "Well, I don't know, six weeks from next Sunday, I just might feel like the fish." Debra and I argue over whether the Atlantic beaches are better than the Pacific beaches and having recently committed to L.A., I vote for the Pacific. We are sitting on some rocks when a stranger asks us where one can meet women on Long Island. We don't know. Debra lives in the city, and I live in L.A. She needs to tell us that she lost her partner, they'd been together ten years. What are the odds? Single solitary deaths happen to everyone. It's the strangest sensation on a day we spend revisiting the memories of the dead. We walk the beach and the only gifts I can offer are two stones, one black, and one white. I walk on in the miraculous gray.

❀

I dream my mother is driving while I sit on the passenger side staring out the window at the clouds. I think I see Jesus, but it's a mirage, like that picture my grandmother has of Jesus and La Virgen de Guadalupe, and depending on the angle, each one comes into focus separately. When will I be done feeling like something is missing, I ask? When the clouds disappear, the rain stops, the grass stops growing, and the sun burns out.

14.

Every time we lose some of our badges of absolute distinction, by which we conferred upon our humanity the right to hold itself apart from its surroundings, it gives us a shock of humiliation.

Rabindranath Tagore, *Sadhana*

May 2005. I take another long walk down a long dirt road, Texas County Road 2391. I took some time off to visit family, and I'm getting some exercise in with my Tía Maggie. She wonders if she dreamed of ever having a baby girl child named Connie—if it actually happened. Only on the anniversary of their deaths, after all this time, do we feel the protracted resurfacing of memory. I don't think of Connie as much. They died within moments of each other as if one were coaxing the other to come to paradise and play. And off they went. That's my childhood version of what happened. In reality, they died in an open field or maybe they died in the ambulance or when they arrived at the hospital. I don't know for sure. No one does, except the hospital, but I asked one year too late because St. Charles Hospital gets rid of the records after fifteen years.

Tía Maggie and I walk faster. My aunt breathes deep for full effect, she likes to sweat when she exercises. "Did I ever tell you about the owl," she asks me. "A week after the girls disappeared," she tells me, "We get home late one night to find an owl sitting on the stairwell inside the house."

That's what we call them now, the girls, for they are now one entity, sewn together in death. And that's what we call their deaths, a "disappearance." Memories cross-fade between families, and we borrow and steal details from each other.

"Oh my God, what is an owl doing in the house, who left the windows open?" she recounts. Nobody. And then she tells me that it took an hour to get the owl out of the house. The owls were a discovery, something my aunt might not have known about her child because she had four others. After going through Connie's school belongings, they found owls and owls, drawings of owls everywhere. The last one was dated one week before her death.

We make it to the end of the road and turn around when we reach the two black cows who have for some reason charged the barbed wire fence. The profound regret in my aunt's voice at having scooted her Connie out of the house with a broom replaces her concerted effort to get a good workout.

Memoria of Maggie Rodriguez

On the day of the accident, I must have not felt very happy that day. I suspected my husband was having an affair with my baby sister Patricia. I did not like my thoughts and feelings about it. It scrambled everything else in my brain. It's funny what pops into your mind sometimes, old memories and strange thoughts when you least expect them.

Connie was going to make her first communion and in order for her to be prepared, I would have to drive her all the way to Bono for her catechism class. The reason I took her and not your uncle was because there was an hour where we would have to wait, and I didn't want your Tío to go and wait at my mom's house where he would be seeing my sister. So, I committed to taking Connie myself. I remember this because it turned into a special time between us. When you have five children, there is never any time to have experiences with just one at a time. On the way home I asked Connie if she believed in Jesus, and she right away says yes. And I go on to ask if she knew what it meant to make her First Communion and she says yes. I was very proud of her, and I want to believe that I was close to her. I made her a dress, and I was so proud of that dress, not knowing that two weeks later we would be burying her in it.

The day the girls died; your Tío Manuel was taking them to your Tía Eva's house for Rachel's pajama party. The girls were very excited and wanted to ride in the back of the pickup truck. I really didn't want them to sit in the back and your Tío and I went back and forth about it because it made me so uncomfortable. But your Tío said it would be OKAY, so they did. Five minutes later, they are back because your Tío forgot his lunch and then came back again because he had forgotten his work boots. The second time Connie got down from the truck and burned her leg or her arm, I don't remember. She was crying and so I suggested she stay with me instead, but she insisted she was fine and wanted to go. I don't remember when, but you decided to get out of the truck and stay. When they were going to leave again, I suggested again to your Tío to have the girls ride in the front of the truck with Patricia and Peggy, but he said they would be fine and that made the girls happy, so I finally let it alone.

I walked to my friend Rosa's house just down the street since my brother was there and all of you kids were playing football. I found out that my dad had been trying to call me, but I was sitting on the front porch talking to Rosa, who always helped me by listening to me even though I'm sure I was always repeating myself. All this time passes and I'm thinking the girls are at Eva's. When I was walking home, my dad and my brother Joe drive by on the way to my house. They tell me there has been an accident, and I have to go with them to the hospital. Rosa went to take care of you and the boys so I could go to the hospital. I prayed all the way to the hospital. When we got to the hospital is when I found out that Connie and Gina had died on impact. A nun took me in to see Connie, but I couldn't believe she was gone. A part of me had died right there, along with my child and I think the Lord took over something in me that allowed me to continue breathing. No one can prepare you for that kind of feeling.

When I saw Connie, I remembered my secret awful thought, and I asked her to forgive me, that was not what I wanted to happen. My thought was for something else, like for the police to stop Tío to tell him that it was not legal for the girls to ride in an open pickup truck, but in Ohio, it was not illegal at that time. I cried so hard holding my daughter, asking her to forgive me for having such bad thoughts. I have learned a lesson, not to think bad thoughts when I'm angry or sad. It seemed like I was only with her for a few minutes, and I didn't know any better than to ask the doctor if I could stay longer.

I don't really remember things in detail. We are not people of detail. Your Tío and I grieved in our own way, not really thinking of the other. I can't even say how my other children dealt with this. I was a stay-at-home mom, but mentally and emotionally I was not there. Of course, I didn't see this until my children are grown and out of the house. That's when I could see where I went wrong. My children have told me that I did a good job in their upbringing, but I wish now that I would have handled things better. Your mom, Tío, and I made arrangements, and got the caskets, but it was decided on the first day of the showing that Gina would not be viewed because she was too swollen, and it didn't look like our Gina.

When the accident that took the girl's life happened, I was beside myself. Only a little later was I grateful for the nine years God gave us with her. He gave us time to get to know Connie and Gina and make memories. I don't remember too much about the funeral. There were a lot of people at the funeral, and I know we were there, but I don't remember a thing about it. All that time I was in la-la land. I remember hearing that everyone was concerned about me because I was the weak one and your mom was the strong one. Mom and Dad were giving me a lot of attention, but I don't remember it. Actually, I believe it was your mom who shared this with me some time ago. I felt bad because I was not aware of it and wished I could have been there for her.

Peggy was 14, Jo-Jo was 13, Eddie-Boy was 12, Connie was 9 and Israel was 8 years old. There was a memorial at Connie's school done by her 3rd-grade teacher, Mr. Rex, who she had a crush on. One day, she didn't want to go to school, and I found out during the parent/teacher conference that it was because she had gotten in trouble for talking out of turn. Her feelings were crushed. After Connie died, the school offered an award for one 6th grader every year who demonstrated the same qualities that she possessed. She was always smiling and very caring for others. She was a little different than the other kids in school. Gina was, too, come to think of it now. For example, there was this one little girl that had been burned badly when she was younger, and kids made fun of her. Connie made friends with her. For many years we would all go to the school and give out the award. When Wynn Elementary got a new principal, he wanted to get rid of the memorial but Mrs. Pastor, another teacher at the school, argued that a memorial is never taken away so to this day, there is an award in Connie's name at Wynn Elementary in Oregon, Ohio.

After the funeral, I went to pick up Connie's belongings from school and noticed that she had drawn an owl on the cover of her folder. She had owls inside too. I never knew she loved owls. I knew she loved cats. A year later, Peggy and Frank were living with us, and one morning as I was coming out of our bedroom, an owl was on the railing in the middle room upstairs. I very quietly opened the door to our room to tell your Tío and then walk to the next room to tell Peggy and Frank. Frank comes out of the bedroom with a gun, for some reason he was confused. We all go downstairs following the owl and your Tío and Frank are trying to get this owl out of the house. It's strange how sometimes we think we know everything there is to know about our children. But since I had four others, I guess I couldn't give each one everything they needed all the time. It seems like I should have known about those owls. My mind likes to think it was her that day, sitting on the stairwell, frustrated that we couldn't see her. We're running around the house like idiots, and it wasn't till much later that I was convinced she came to visit.

Time passed and one day I decided I wanted to look at my daughter every day, so I put her picture in a frame and placed it on a shelf at the end of the upstairs hallway. I then added Gina's picture and some flowers, and then I added a candle, not realizing that I was putting together my own little memorial. Looking at them every morning is something I did for myself. It's the only thing I could do. The only thing there is to do is to create something, anything to help fill up the empty space.

15.

Make no mistake about this, my
beloved brothers: all we are given
is good, and all our endowments
are faultless, descending from above,
from the Father of heavenly lights,
who knows no change of rising and setting,
who casts no shadow on the earth.

Epistle of James 1:16-17

The truck flipped vertically over its front end more than once and into an open field. It was a field like all the fields of my childhood. During car rides, I would stare at the neatly cultivated mounds of dirt in perfect rows and try to count them until I fell into a trance or fell asleep. Connie was found close to the truck; Gina was thrown farther away—her leg bent back and twisted to the side, a narrow stream of blood flowing from the corner of her mouth. Did they feel it? Did my sister feel herself flying from the truck, landing crooked? Did the girls speak to each other in the in-between place? It took me twenty years to think of asking how it happened. I have no idea why it took me that long to want to know and no idea why my aunt hadn't told anyone else till then.

I was in grad school, sitting on the floor in my dining room talking to my Tía Patricia on the phone. At the time of the accident, she was sixteen years old, the youngest girl of eleven children (my mom being the oldest) and sitting inside the cab of the truck taking the girls to my cousin Rachel's pajama party. My aunt Patricia now has three kids of her own, as does my cousin Rachel. I'm staring out the large window that looks onto the desert landscape behind my apartment building finally asking her what actually happened. I didn't plan on asking, it just occurred to me somehow. She tells me about the open field, Gina's bent leg, the blood. She tells me that my uncle went crazy, and my cousin Peggy was in shock, screaming and running around trying to find her sister Connie. My young aunt Patricia goes in search of my sister. I imagine it over and over again, as if the whole story is brand new as if it just happened. I imagine my sister flying out of the truck, seeing the ground below and the sky above before landing. How far was that? She flew too far for us to have an open casket, that's how far.

A tiny bit of information can change everything. I no longer have the luxury of childhood thoughts preventing me from imagining the truth of it. I used to imagine the acrobatics, the flying. I imagined heaven and all the ice cream and oranges she could eat. It wasn't until much later that I imagine the paramedics walking into the field, lifting them onto gurneys, and then putting both of them in the ambulance. Did they die on impact? My aunt says she heard my sister moan. Maybe they died before ever arriving at the hospital, and the paramedics simply offered the gift of hope for a little while longer. I decided to get out of the truck that would eventually crash into another car and kill my sister and cousin on their way to a pajama party, a party I was supposed to attend. At the last minute, I got out of the truck.

In Buddhism, for every cause, there is an effect. This is Law. The effect is exponential and for some reason, one day, I think I'm going to understand why this happened, but I haven't yet.

March 2002. Love is bending me and making me wish for a life of desert afternoons. I'm in Tucson getting my wits about me after having left New York, and before moving to Los Angeles. I am in a state of non-permanency, just like my relationship. For the time being, C is furious at life. She has decided that it's now okay to take up space in this world and everyone should just get the fuck out of her way. Roxanne has given us her casita as temporary space and we are grateful, but I'm too old to live in a studio apartment and would rather pay money for a bathroom that isn't in the kitchen. I move to the barrio, where I will edit my thesis film. It's hot. It's vacant. I become the slow, immovable planet Saturn while C becomes Pluto, the furthest planet from Earth. She does circles around me, spinning out of control. Doubt will become such a constant companion that the idea of listening to it slowly fades until I'm left with a perpetual barely noticeable low-grade anxiety that follows me wherever I go.

My friends rally around my ridiculous transitory situation. Roxanne comes over and builds me a rustic corner desk from plywood so I can finish editing my thesis film. And she allows me the use of her beautiful mission-style bed. She is a sculptor by training and now a landscape designer who can build anything in about ten minutes. She helps me rebuild myself in about twenty. All my crap is in storage, so

Kim buys me a gorgeous blender, which makes drinking margaritas one of the truly satisfying things about life. My best friend Barbara buys me a set of mid-century dishes from St. Vincent DePaul that remind me of haikus because of the delicate chicken scratch patterns in light blue and mustard. I will change my heart after this year's monsoons. I decide I will get out of New York permanently, and move to Los Angeles when I feel like it, which, right now, is never. The desert is a place where I learn everything, I need to know about myself. It's where I learn that almost always, it is best to surrender. The desert is starkly beautiful, an "abundance of absence," is the way Rebecca Solnit describes it. I am stripped of excess; I am stripped of the privilege of holding on to too much. I drink margaritas and eat on haikus.

One of the strangest qualities about tragic events in the past is the way they turn into weirdly comforting mysteries in the present, particularly in light of a more current hardship. You are capable of seeing the gaps and spaces of the past with more clarity when subtle but deep healing is taking place. One winter night after my sister's death, the world was white with snow and the smell of our fireplace filled me up, like-breathing through an inhaler when you're sick. I realize I'm grateful to my mother for not asking me why I want to chop wood when it's snowing. Or why I want the fan on while pressed underneath heavy blankets. Or for not asking me why I want to mow the entire lawn with a push mower when we have a riding mower. Or why I sometimes like sitting in the linen closet. Or why I sometimes like reading on the stairs.

Death experienced by children who are too old to be clueless, but too young to know what to do, must count as something unique. There is this "sense that what you're going through is all too strange to be pure chance; it's such a peculiar set of circumstances that it can only be God's will," says Dave Eggers. I decide that this must make me special somehow, and I will wear it like a shield. It was a subtle decision; one I didn't realize I'd made until my handy shield prevented people from getting too close to me. After all, they might suddenly disappear, and I should therefore be cautious.

In "The Destiny of Borges" philosopher Enrique Mari asks Borges about the enigma of truth and the enigma of death. He responds:

> For me death is a hope, the irrational certitude of being abolished, erased, and forgotten. When I'm sad, I think, what does it matter what happens to a twentieth-century South American writer? What do I have to do with all of this? You think it matters what happens to me now, if tomorrow I will have disappeared? I hope to be totally forgotten. I believe that this is death. Yet perhaps I'm wrong, and what follows is another life on another plane, no less interesting than this one, and I will accept that life too, just as I have accepted this one.

Perhaps it is my new-age mind that has always been attracted to this notion of other planes of existence, or maybe it's what accounts for my interest in science and science fiction. When I first went to college, I was especially fascinated with molecular biology and became a pre-med major. I was so certain that this was my path because even as early as junior high, I carried an illustrated anatomy book to all my classes. I had a special fondness for the anatomy of the heart and would explain to my friend Beth how fitting it is that the heart has four chambers (like St. Theresa's four waters) and proceed to show her the bloody details of it in my book. After my third year of pre-med, and the impossible feat of getting through organic chemistry and neurobiology, I realized my mind was not suited to the task of science. I went to my neurobiology professor's office during hours and explained how confused I was. "How can I possibly get a D on my first quiz when this is the most fascinating class, I've ever taken in my entire college career? How can I love it and not do well?" I asked. He smiled at me, reminding me that this was an advanced split-level class. "But I'm advanced," I said, pleading. I think he was amused. He told me to hang in there and showed me how to study for his quizzes. Slowly, my scores increased, little by little. It was excruciating. By the final exam, I had to score an A- in order to get a B in the class. I did it, just to prove to myself that I could, and then I dropped out of science without a bit of regret.

I graduated with a double-major degree in Molecular Biology and English and a minor in Media Arts. Needless to say, I was going to have to focus, or was I? The worlds of art, imagination, and science will continue to collide for me and playfully coexist throughout my graduate career and into the world of business where I will learn the art of collaboration, acceleration, and co-creation. I didn't know then what a tagline this could be for the rest of my life. I will never find myself explaining with ease what it is I'm good at.

My mother and I are standing in front of a large scroll of translucent paper, a beating heart. By firelight, my mother moves her fingers down to a name. I can see for miles behind me through darkness, a tiny lamp in the corner of my mind's eye. We've lost our way, I say. But my mother denies oblivion. Here, she says, she is right here, for always. I look at the name and it burns off the page.

Photo: Victoria (left), Virginia (right), 1969

Photo: Victoria (left), Virginia (right), 1977

16.

Recognize what is before your eyes, and what is
hidden will be revealed to you.

The Gospel of Thomas

I have no way of recreating the accident in my mind since I wasn't
there. I have no way of re-creating the hospital or the timeline of
events over and over again—to get it straight in my head. One minute
I waved goodbye, and then she was gone. She just disappeared. I
never saw her again. Not at the hospital, not at the funeral. Never.
And it's true, I've learned, that it's quite normal to believe she is
coming back. Any day now, she'll just show up.

On the first anniversary of her death, my mom and I created a photo
album and stenciled her name on the front—Virginia Marie Garza,
October 31, 1968—May 19, 1978. At the end of this exercise, as I
flipped through the pictures it occurred to me that it was my photo
album too since I'm in every picture. I've also learned that it's true,
for who knows how long, that when you are no longer in mourning

but still grieving you walk around in a state that can best be described as "cloud cover." I still cannot remember anything that happened to me for three years after the accident. I'm sure I laughed and felt happy, but the memories of that period are not at all clear. The marker left is absolutely definitive. My months of May are an incessant light wind that blows me open and leaves me exposed to weepy weather.

May 19, 2008. Park Slope, Brooklyn. I've flown in from L.A. to shoot documentary footage in the city and am back at Lori and Jerry's, clicking through my email while Lori eats lunch, watching the cooking channel. Lori and her older sister Lisa have a beautiful relationship, and I model my sister's fantasy on them. They collaborate creatively, go camping, have dinner parties, do each other favors, share a car, and cheer each other on in every way. Yes, like that. Of course, it's easier to fantasize about a sister who is dead because there are no real-life issues souring our perfectly constructed relationship. Of course, in my mind, my sister and I are the best of pals, and we talk every day, take vacations together, and share recipes, and she is always there for me. She can never leave me because she's family. She is basically stuck with me. She doesn't have a profession. Her job is to be my sister and be there for me at all times. And she is an excellent sister, forever.

I believed people when they told me it would just take time. In time, I would feel better. Well, of course, I do. In fact, feeling bad is not the correct way to say it. Empty is better. Yes. Empty. And yet, not one of these people ever told me about the obliterating waves of sadness that strike, like lightning over dinner when someone casually asks if I have any siblings. What do I say? This question has always puzzled me. I've never known what to say. If I say, yes, but she's dead, then it sounds like I am suffering some prolonged mental illness especially after they realize how long ago it was. The D-word causes abrupt silences and makes me feel like a major buzzkill. If I say no, then it obliterates the fact that she ever existed, which is equally unacceptable. Yes, I had a sibling for nine years and in that time, I developed an everlasting, unbreakable relationship that will shadow me forever, pass the potatoes, please. But you can't get into all that with a casual question, so I answer depending on my mood. Yes, but she was killed in a car accident when I was very young. Or no, I have no siblings.

May 2010. My mom's friend Patricia Karmol, who was there during the entire tragedy, emails me on the anniversary of my sister's death to let me know she's thinking of me. I tell her I'm writing a book. She offers me her memories. I will learn that when my mother arrived at the hospital, a priest led her down a hallway, and all of a sudden, my mother cried out, "Oh no!" The door closed and there was silence. I will learn that my mother took a picture of my sister in case she decided on a closed casket. I never knew about this picture and have never seen it. I will learn that Pat's mother did our laundry and ironed my mother's funeral clothes. I will learn that our neighbors from across the street, the Ronstadts, came to our house and finished cutting the grass that my mother left unfinished. I will learn that my mother confided in Patricia that she felt something was going to happen a week before it did. I will learn that the morning my sister died, my mom was backing out of the driveway on her way to work when Gina motioned for her to stop and come back. My mother gets out of the car and goes to the door where my sister is standing. My sister hugs her tightly for the last time and kisses her goodbye. I will learn that angels disguised as real people exist in everyday life.

Gina and Connie were uncannily alike. After their death, the family mythology could not imagine just one of them surviving. If one died the other had to die too, it only made sense. We accepted it, and perhaps it was comforting to make meaning out of facts, observations, and incidents that otherwise would've remained untied, unknown, or uncared for, meaningless. We can't help but create meaning because we need to feel sewn into the fabric of something larger than ourselves. As a child, I felt safe, or rather I didn't need to feel safe because I had nothing else to compare it to. I never felt threatened. I think this is called security. When you grow up feeling secure, and then suffer the shock of threat, you only have two choices: 1) you can live without fear because you learn that all things are impermanent, and beyond your control, or 2) you can live with immense fear because all things are impermanent, and beyond your control. For a long time, I felt safe in the thought that my family had fulfilled its sacrificial quota—the gods devoured two nine-year-old girls. Surely, they were sated. We were safe. Death could move on.

Two weeks before her death, we went to Defiance, Ohio to visit some friends. During our visit, my sister made fast friends with a young girl her same age, the daughter of a couple we'd all just met that day. They became such good friends that by the end of the day, my sister begged and pleaded to stay the night at her new friend's house. I tried to tell her mom wouldn't go for it, because it was a Saturday and tomorrow was Sunday and we were not going to drive all the way back to Defiance just to pick her up. The final answer was, "No, not this time but we'll be back in two weeks, and you can stay over then." My sister insisted that the next time she saw her friend it would be in heaven. I dismissed her plea as an exaggeration, which she was always prone to. I sighed and looked at my mother with a "what are we going to do with her" look on my face, reminding my sister that it was "only two weeks

away, which is fourteen days because there are seven days in a week."
But she was right. Two weeks later, she died.

One year later, when I was in Mrs. Johnson's fifth-grade class, we shared camp with the fifth-grade class of Defiance, Ohio. I'd forgotten all about her, that girl, my sister's friend, two weeks before her death, until I saw her. My heart froze and I was paralyzed with excitement, but also fear. I suppressed the urge to run to her and hug her tightly. Instead, I watched her. She was walking by herself near some picnic tables. She was holding a stick and making marks where she walked. I found the courage to walk over to her and start a conversation, something like, "Do you like the weather class?" Every morning we had to walk up a large steep hill to a small, prefabricated structure to take a class about the weather. How are clouds formed? What is lightning? Why does it snow? I really enjoyed this class because I was in awe that one could measure something as vast as the weather.

But the girl did not recognize me. I couldn't tell if she was exuding such sadness or if I was painting that picture of her. For all I knew, she could've been ecstatic inside herself. I really wanted her to remember me, to remember my sister with me. I got a knot in my throat and before I could talk myself out of it, I kept asking her stupid questions. I was so excited about the possibility that we could share the memory of my sister that I talked myself into another trap. I forgot to consider that I would have to tell her Gina was dead. I dared myself anyway but failed to connect and must admit I was both relieved and disappointed. I walked away.

My mother is making a campfire. She teaches me to arrange the sticks in such a way as to let air pass through and underneath them. Fire needs air. We hold hands and watch the flame get bigger. I look up at her and a tear is running down her face. I don't want her to see that I've noticed because it's the only thing I have to offer, so I look back at the fire, and inside the flames, my sister prays for us.

17.

Nature and God—I neither knew
Yet Both so well knew me
They startled, like Executors
of My identity

Emily Dickinson, "Nature and God—I neither knew"

After our parents separated, we would spend weekends with our father. We would go from our two-story white house in the country to Piccadilly East Apartments, which was right next to a freeway, but where at the very least they had a basketball court. We would trudge our bags, toys, and book to our dad's apartment for fun, freedom, and sugar-filled weekends, crashing on Sunday nights just as we arrived back home. It was nice while it lasted. After the divorce was final, my father moved back to his hometown in Texas, and shortly after that, he came back to Ohio for his younger daughter's funeral.

My father has a tattoo of my sister's name on his arm, which he admitted was acquired during a drunken grief-stricken evening of self-pity. He also has a peculiar penchant for being able to remember, in detail, our early childhood years, but after my sister's death, a gaping hole of nothingness. For nine years after Gina died, my relationship with him was intermittent at best. It was not for lack of love; in fact, I'd always been capable of nothing but love for my father, despite his drinking and not paying the child support. He seemed to me, even as a young person, to be my friend, and because I was so well-loved by my mother, I didn't take his issues personally. My mother seemed to understand this and kept her criticism of him to a minimum. Perhaps this was due to her integrity, or she was just being practical. When you are the only parent around, you are the only one your child can rebel against. However, when my mother drew the line, she drew it hard.

A year or maybe two after my sister died, I have an opportunity to go to Texas with my Tío Manual and Tía Maggie to visit my dad. I want to go, but out of nowhere, I break out in hives the day before I'm supposed to leave on the trip. My mother decides right then that I'm not going. I'm furious at her, and when she tries to explain why she doesn't feel right about my going, I accuse her of trying to keep me away from my father and throw in some other assorted divorced kid crap. I have welts all over my body, and I'm crying a river on the kitchen floor, bawling like the grown child I am. My mother is unmoved.

Perhaps she remembers the time she let me go off with my dad one afternoon when we went to Texas to visit. My dad and I had spent the afternoon at his favorite bar, me shooting pool and drinking Shirley Temples and him sitting at the bar drinking his brewskies and talking about how great I am. Of course, the trick is to give your kid an endless supply of all the Temples they can drink, and an endless supply of quarters for the jukebox and pool table. When I got hungry my dad just had the bartender make me fresh hot French fries. Of course, my father lost track of time. When we finally got back to the house, my mother was standing in the driveway with her arms crossed. To suggest that my mother was upset does not come close. My Tío Edward (mom's youngest brother) was standing with her and looked like he could knock my dad out. I thought of running interference and told her immediately what a great time I had, but she didn't care if I was playing pool with La Virgin de Guadalupe herself. She told me to get inside the house and I hugged my dad tight, wishing him luck before doing as I was told.

The next day, when my hives are gone, I walk quietly over to my mother who is sitting at the kitchen table reading *The Toledo Blade,* and say, "Look, my welts are gone," when what I mean is, maybe I didn't want to go as much I thought I did. Look at that, she says, kissing me, when what she means is, I'm the parent and I know what's best for you. She smacks my butt and asks me to take out the garbage.

It is early 1988, during my sophomore year in college when I receive a phone call from my dad's sister, Tía Janey, in the middle of the night, telling me that my dad is in a coma and not expected to live. I handle it well, considering it was his third admittance into the hospital that year and everyone expected it to be his last, everyone but me. I call my mom and ask her to meet me in San Antonio because I cannot see my way to handling my dad's side of the family by myself. My grandmother Ama Mela is the wailing and fainting type. She fainted in the driveway of our house during a family reunion one summer. I was peeking in between my mother's legs to catch a glimpse of her. I felt a trickle of sweat on the back of my mother's knee where I was holding on and a light wind on my face from the fan my mom had fashioned out of a section of *The Toledo Blade*, "She just needs some air, give her some air," my mom said with authority. "She'll be fine, this happened last summer, recuerdas?" added my dad. But I thought she was dying, so I monitored her chest in case it stopped rising and falling slowly. My aunt rushed back with a wet washcloth. When my grandmother came to, she said she was overcome with happiness, and then told my dad to go get her another beer.

The strange reality is that it feels like time has stopped for everyone but me. I am still Vicky who spent the summers of her childhood in Texas with my dad's side, who loved firecrackers, riding bicycles, swimming till I wrinkled, tortillas without butter, and bomb pops. I was sometimes bossy and sometimes a "little miss knows it all." I am still my father's daughter, and my grandmother is still going to offer me money to buy candy, regardless of my age.

No one expects my father to "pull out of it." What does that mean? That is what everyone keeps saying, a warning, "He may not pull out of it," or "It will be a miracle if he pulls out of it." We fill out paperwork because I'm entitled to veteran's benefits since my father was in the Air Force. I explain to the lady, who's sitting across from my mother and me, at a disheveled desk, which is probably not her desk, but rather a temporary, rotating space for the several people who get paid very little money to fill this part of their job. She looks like she's dying to have a smoke. "I want my mother to get the money instead," I tell her. "If my dad doesn't pull out of it."

But to everyone's surprise, my father does "pull himself out" of the darkness called death in a VA hospital and is moved from Intensive Care to a normal room. A day later he wakes up and the first thing he asks is, "What did you do to your hair?" "What do you know about hair anyway?" I snap back. It was the 80s and I had the wildly popular asymmetrical cut where one side was longer than the other. A day after that he's begging me to sneak him up some ice cream sandwiches. And I do because regardless of what the nurses say, an ice cream sandwich isn't going to kill him. That is the year our real relationship begins, and the first year I'm terrified he's going to die at any moment.

18.

People who do not intuit or respect the laws of acceleration and momentum break bones; those who do not grasp the principles of love waste their lives and break their hearts.

Thomas Lewis, M.D., Fari Amini, M.D., Richard Lannon, M.D.:
A *General Theory of Love*

Patricia (Trisha) is the youngest daughter in her family, my mother's youngest sister. She taught me how to ride a bike, play softball, and dance ("the cool way, like black people"). She taught me to be strong, confident, and fearless. When she got her driver's license, she taught me how to drive. In the summer, when the family would gather at Pearson Park for barbecues and softball, she and I would steal off and go driving through the park. She had just started smoking an occasional cigarette, which is why she would convince my sister to stay behind and play—otherwise everyone in the family would know about her indiscretion. She would give me an abbreviated driving lesson and off we went, cruising, she called it. And to sound more grown-up, she would add a Spanglish word here and there for effect.

While in high school, she and my Tía Maria would play Marvin Gaye and Smokey Robinson albums and secretly smoke pot in the upstairs bedroom.

Every few years, the three youngest kids would change rooms. The bedroom at the top of the stairs used to be Maria's when she had painted it in rainbow colors and listened to Donny Osmond. Ed was in the middle room, while Trisha was in a corner room that she had painted red. She had red shag carpet, red curtains, and red satin sheets. When they all switched rooms, each room would be transformed to reflect their newfound maturity. Ed was my hero. My grandmother would use him to get me to do anything she wanted. If Ed ate his vegetables, I would eat my vegetables. If he took naps, I would take naps. Once, when I realized he was just pretending to be taking a nap and was not in the room at all, I snuck out the window onto the roof, down the antennae ladder on the side of the house and made a run for the park down the street. After an hour I came back, but my grandmother was waiting by the door. Eventually, I realized that it was not in my best interest to defy my grandmother, and not because she would punish me, in fact, quite the opposite. She would turn silent, and the look on her face was enough for me to want to avoid the shame I'd feel for having disobeyed her.

It was Patricia's job to debunk the myths plaguing Gina and me. She took it as her job to wrench us from our innocence and anoint us into the world of adults (even though she was fifteen). It was her mission to explain why there was no Santa Claus or Easter bunny and why these were necessary lies. She explained to me what civil rights were, and why black people were better at most everything. I interrupted her, "Like at the Baptist church Mom took us to where everyone was a good singer, and everyone could play instruments?" I asked.

Gina and I had been puzzled when we were told to bring our own instruments to Trina's church one Sunday. We can take instruments to church, I asked. Trina was my mother's co-worker and friend at the Ohio State Welfare and Social Work Agency. Her two sons, Harvey and Cash would be there and had instruments of their own. I was overwhelmed by having to choose which one to bring since we had a basket full of them, maracas, triangles, little drums, and tambourines. I decided on my red Mexican maracas and pleaded with my mother to let me take the tambourine, as well. My sister chose a small triangular string instrument. We were standing on the pew playing our instruments like mad girls, working up a sweat and singing our guts out, and we screamed with glee, beside ourselves when the nice smelling woman in front of us bellowed out "Praise Jesus!" while we hysterically bobbed up, and I paused for a second fearing jumping on the pew would be going a step too far but something had come over us, and we were filled with an indescribable joy, something like madness, and we loved everyone and everyone loved us—thank you, God; thank you, Jesus; thank you, everyone! The preacher thanked us for coming, and as we walked to our car, I told my mother I wanted to be a Baptist. You can't be a Baptist, Mija, you are a Catholic, she said. I really wanted to be Baptist. I really want to be Baptist too, said my sister, and we sang our Baptist hearts out all the way home.

Patricia also explained the difference between Republicans and Democrats. She explained the various terms related to one's sexual parts and why it's so not cool to call your vagina a vagina. "Look, if I take the first two letters out of vagina...I get Gina!" My sister did not think that was funny. Although when my mother found out that she had taught us to call our breasts boobies, titties or anthills, Patricia was scolded. My mother didn't want us using disrespectful nicknames for our body parts. Patricia explained why it's good to masturbate and which sins are really sins and which are just made-up, old-fashioned ideas (but forbade us to tell our mom). She explained why prostitutes "work hard for the money," in that song by Donna Summer. She explained why rock-n-roll is essential for survival and why Aretha Franklin "is and always will be the most important female vocalist ever." Then, on May 19, 1978, my sixteen-year-old Tía Patricia was sitting in a field crying, holding her niece and reassuring her that everything would be okay.

Memoria of Patricia Resendez

I was staying at your house for most of pretty much that year. I helped get you girls off to school and be there for you when you got home. Sometimes I would stay the weekend, or whenever your mom needed me. I remember on Thursday you girls were so excited to be going to Rachel's party the following day after school. I don't remember how we got to Maggie's, but right before we were going to leave for the party you flung yourself out of the truck and ran into the yard and yelled you were going to stay there. I asked you if you were sure, and you said yes and then you went off to play with Eddie-Boy. I remember your Tía Maggie and Manuel exchanging words about the girls sitting in the back of the truck. Maggie really didn't want them to, but Manuel reassured Maggie that he would take the back roads and go very slowly. We told the girls where to sit and that they should sit close together crouched near the cab of the truck. They had begged to sit in the back and were very pleased when they were allowed, smiling from ear to ear.

It was a warm ordinary day in May, very sunny. We were very excited to be driving inside that truck because it was an older model truck and we thought we looked cool. All three of us, your cousin Peggy, your Tío Manuel, and I were constantly looking back at the girls to make sure they were still sitting down. We traveled from Stadium Road to Wynn Road. The speed limit on Wynn Road, I believe, was only 35mph and Manuel was not even close to that limit. I remember reaching the intersection and being hit. I want to say that I thought the car was going to stop, but it all happened very quickly. Manuel tried to maintain control, but the impact sent us off into the field, flipping over. I don't know for sure, but we seemed to flip at least three times. It felt like forever, as if everything was going in slow motion, I was able to hear every sound of the impact wishing and wondering when we would stop. We landed with the tires on the ground, and Manuel immediately asked if we were okay. Peggy, immediately after the impact, was screaming and crying, and Manuel was very nervous and crying, his hands constantly moving with every thought that was going through his mind. We all got out and started stumbling around looking for the girls.

Manuel found Connie by the truck, and I kept calling out for Gina, looking everywhere around the truck, but I was not able to see her. It seemed like forever but could only have been a minute or maybe two before I found her by the side of the road. She was lying on her back with a trickle of blood coming from her mouth and her leg was unnaturally positioned. She groaned. I held her and kept reassuring her that she was going to be okay, and that help was coming, to hold on. She was unconscious. It was probably ten or fifteen minutes before the ambulance arrived, at least it seemed like forever. Peggy and Manuel were together once they found Connie, while I was with Gina. I continued to hold her in my arms until the ambulance got there. I just kept looking at her and saying the same thing over and over again. I didn't know what else to do, I was only sixteen years old. The next thing I remember we are waiting in the police car, and I kept trying to get out, but they wouldn't let me. We were told that the police car would take us to the hospital. Manuel came to the car before we left and reassured us that we were going to follow the girls to the hospital. Peg and I cried in each other's arms but believed the whole time that the girls were going to be fine.

We were all waiting in a family waiting room while the girls were being checked out. I remember Maggie telling me through her tears that she was glad that I was there for Connie, in her absence. After your mom arrived, they allowed them to go see the girls. We were not allowed to go in. I am the youngest girl in our family, and there were my two oldest sisters, crying with one another. I was seeing everybody as if in a dream. I thought this had to be a dream, like a lucid dream, and that it could not actually be happening. I cannot remember how long we were at the hospital before they told us the girls had not made it. They died only four minutes apart. I cannot remember which one died first. Your mother knew what she had to do, and she seemed to take the lead, which was so amazing to me at the time. In hindsight, she did not give herself the time to openly mourn and freak out. Not then anyway.

I was asked several times if I was hurt. The lower side under my right shoulder was sore so they checked me out, and it was only a deep scratch, not anything that required stitches, but it was deep enough to leave a scar. I remember going home with my mom, and her making me some Yerbaniz (herbal tea) to calm my nerves and fears. She slept with me for about a week because I kept having nightmares and would cry a lot in the middle of the night.

The funeral was very emotional. I remember us girls (Mary, Peg, and I) sitting together and my and Mary's best friend Carol sitting in the pews behind us. I remember the family, the brothers being very supportive and loving. The family had never felt closer to me, actually. The feeling of so much love all around, in the midst of so much sorrow and tears, is something I remember, but find so difficult to explain.

I was very close to you girls because I was still quite young myself, but old enough to be a responsible aunt. I remember that we would go bike riding a lot together. I would make sure you girls did your homework after school, even though Gina was always on top of it. Then we would go outside and play different games and things. We would walk to Reno Beach, just down the street, and watch TV together until your mom came home from work. I remember when Elvis died, the three of us were watching TV, and Gina says she's not afraid to die. That stuck with me because Robbie her friend had recently died. Robbie lived close to Rachel and every time you guys went to visit, he would come over. I think he loved her. He was playing with his brothers in the church rectory, and they were riding an old elevator without walls that went up to a second-floor room. He wasn't paying attention and broke his neck. It was so horrible. I remember Gina being so very sad about it. I remember looking at her and she reassured me that she was not going to die yet. But the word "yet" always stuck out in my mind, especially after she did die.

Strange things go through your mind. I remember the time that Gina got lost at Sears. I thought she was with your mom, and Terry thought that she was with me. We looked and looked and called out her name for what seemed to be an hour. I think your mom found her underneath a clothing rack. The three of us got yelled at. I remember Gina being afraid of Lobo, your dad's pure-bred German Shepherd, and using the broom to scoot the food bowl to him; we would tease her about that. Gina was so beautiful, such an old soul spirit. She would always write notes and leave them for us to find them. I still have one.

It was some time after the accident, I remember sitting at McDonald's with my mom, Mary, and Eddie. I looked right at my mom and told her I thought I needed counseling. I remember her being taken aback because we are not really therapy people. But shortly after that, I was going to therapy. I truly felt that the therapist was not helping me, so after about three sessions, I stopped going. I don't think he took me seriously. I have sought counseling three other times in my adult life. Each time I felt as though my life had gotten too out of control, and I felt a breakdown or meltdown coming. I luckily have been able to come to the conclusion that I needed outside intervention to assist me and get me grounded again. Each time I have found myself at that low place, I've been able to pick myself back up, growing and evolving each time spiritually and emotionally.

My sisters and I were not close when I was a later teen because of the age difference, and due to the secret life I was living with Manuel. I could always tell Maggie wanted to be closer to me, I think because of the accident, and the fact that I had been there for Connie and Peg when she wasn't, but I could not because I was living with this deception. Manuel relied on me a lot after the accident, which inevitably took our relationship to a different and deeper level. I would try to encourage him to go to Maggie, to lean on her, but his guilt was too deep. I became his best friend, and he became mine.

I worry about my three kids a lot because I know death can be only a minute away, I worry too much. I also ask God to prepare me if there is something coming toward me if that is even possible. I think your mom was prepared in a way. My connection with my sisters today is truly a blessing. They each are very special and strong women, and I try to take a bit from each of them and learn to be a better person, a better woman, mother, wife, and sister. I have always wished the same for you and Peggy—to have your sisters near as I've had mine. That you don't have that and never will is one of the saddest and most difficult things for me to accept.

19.

As the massive ocean first casts then absorbs the sun's fading rays, you bounce a bit in your corridor, these thoughts and no others, a fear that what is lacking in your condition is what is required to go on, while you go on.

Barbara Cully, "Three Views of a Sunset in March "

La Misión, Baja California is where I walk on quicksand. The notion of an ocean as a potion is muy attractive. This is where I walk. This is where I cook. This is where Barbara makes margaritas. Very little speaking, relatively speaking, occurs here but nonetheless, it's where everything happens. My relationship with C is over, and while I'm relieved, I'm also in the phase called "This is so unfair." I'm learning over and over again that attachment carries with it the fearsome responsibility of losing things you think you'd rather not do without. It's a foreign country called myself. Mexico is easy. I'm difficult. What I carry with me when I walk is a stick of thoughts that I dig into the sand with every step, hoping I will understand the world better when I get back to the house in time to build a fire. I look at this branch I've found on the beach and am catapulted to the past.

I reach for the branch because it's smooth, which should've been my first clue. I swing and swing and swing and crack. I plummet down to the ground, slowed only by the passing bark, which rips the skin off my back like a cheese grater. My sister screams a piercingly loud animal cry, and my mother appears instantly, nothing broken but my spirit. My mom stretches me across her legs, and I watch my sister's face contort while my mom and aunt wisp away the particles of bark still clinging to my flesh, then apply layers of ointment. I walk out of the house again with my entire back wrapped in gauze. You could've died, my sister says. I'm not going to die from falling out of a tree, I say. Not me.

I want to die a hero, not an idiot.

As I walk the beach, I think of certain moments in my life when I felt spared. Like the time I was on Enid Zentelis' film school shoot at NYU and needed to adjust a light that was situated on the roof because the sun was setting. It was the kind of house in New Jersey that reminded me of Archie and Edith Bunker's place. It's windy and I'm moving too quickly while attempting to adjust the direction of the light, it starts to swing, and rather than just let the light fall, I try and save it, but instead, I fall with it onto the hood of a car one story below. After my landing on the hood instead of the concrete driveway, the ballast ricochets off the pole instead of making minced meat out of my insides. My film school classmates responded like an emergency SWAT team. I'm safely transported to the hospital, where I beg the EMT not to cut my jeans because they are my favorites, and I don't have the money to buy another pair. My neck is in a brace, and I stare at the water-stained ceiling of a poorly lit hospital. I'm fine after nine months of occupational therapy. Small things like finishing my film seem to pale in comparison to getting full use of my left hand.

The accident is a very concrete thing. She did die. But for some reason, I keep thinking there is more to be figured out about this event. It is strange and often feels wrong to weigh her death against any other tragic incidents of mortality. In *Storming the Gates of Paradise*, Solnit says of the tsunami that hit Southeast Asia, "People were still searching for their own children, their own dead, among the many dead, for the tragedy that was personal amid the enormity." The same was true of 9/11 when scores of families posted flyers for their missing people, who almost all turned out to be dead. What am I doing here? Why was I spared? Why did I choose that week to leave New York? Why did I jump out of the truck when the pajama party was something I'd been looking forward to? I tried to go about it like a scientist, calculating, measuring, and recording all the facts. But facts are slippery things. They are shapeshifters, taking forms, expanding or shrinking to suit the occasion, but simultaneously never really losing their essential hardness. Everyone in my family who has any recollection of that sunny day in May remembers things differently. Everyone except my grandmother, Emilia.

At the end of the last day at the funeral home, my mother asks my grandparents to take me to the hearse. I'm sitting between them, and my grandmother presses me tight against her ample body. My hand rests on her leg, and I look at it as if it's detached until she folds it inside her soft palm. I'm caught inside the web of security she spun for me and the feeling of calmness inside my heart is indescribable. The woman who says, "Con favor de Dios" (if God grants us another day)" wraps me in all her history and protects me with her faith.

Memoria of Emilia Resendez

I am twelve years old when I'm asked to take some fresh milk to a woman I will one day know as Tía Jesusa. My father was a farmer and every day they'd milk the cows and have us go and sell the fresh milk to the neighbors. When I get to your grandpa's house, his older sister calls out for her brother Gilbrando, who is seventeen years old, to "Come over here and look at this lovely girl with the most beautiful eyes." I got so embarrassed, my face was very red, I wanted to swallow my head. That was the first time I met your grandfather. I was too young to care for such things and besides, he had tons of girls after him, because he was so handsome, and he was already a young man. When I reached the 8th grade, I had to stop going to school and care for the family because my mother went to work. It was the saddest day of my life because I loved school and I was very good at it. I didn't have any girlfriends to go out with, and I didn't go to parties or anything like that because I was always working at the house, taking care of my sisters and brothers. I was busy all day. I was fifteen-and-a-half years old when I started seeing your grandpa at church. All the girls wanted him, and there were some who would fight over him, but I was too busy to care so I went about my business and didn't pay any attention to him. It's funny cause I'm the one who caught him.

It was 1943 when Gil wrote me a little note, asking me to the movies. He had to ask for my father's permission. I went to the movies, which cost only five cents then, but I had to take all my sisters and brothers with me. Eventually, your grandpa was allowed to come over to the house, and we were going together for a year when my parents decide to split up and get a divorce. It was my mother's doing, she was a real pistol, and she's the one that wanted out of the marriage. When she went to work, I had to stop going to school. My mom wanted to move to Corpus Christi, and Gil didn't want me to go. That's when he asked me to marry him. I told him I didn't want to get married till I was eighteen years old, but then I prayed about it and asked God to give me a sign that if this was the real thing then I would do it. After two weeks of being apart, I knew he was the one. Your grandpa didn't even tell his mom about me. I didn't even know some of his family. He goes home one day and says, "I'm getting married," just like that. Ama Lolita asks him who on God's earth he plans to marry, and how is it that she doesn't even know this girl? He says, "Well, you're going to know her now." You know your grandpa, how he is.

We got married November 25th, 1944. I was going to be seventeen in five months. I think we had thirty-five dollars to our name, but we were young and in love, so we didn't care. We moved around a little bit, trying for better jobs here and there. My grandfather was going to give us two goats, and two pigs to get started on our own farm, but your grandfather didn't want to have anything to do with farming or animals. Later your grandpa settled on a job learning the roofing trade. We bought a tiny house for $125.00, and your grandpa added four rooms and we stayed in that house. Your mom was the first child born there, and then came Margarita, Evangelina, Gilbrando II, then John, Lupita, Joe, Martin, Maria, Patricia, and then finally Eduardo. Most of the kids grew up in that house except for the last three. Ed was about two years old when we moved to Ohio, and Maria and Patricia were young girls.

In Ohio, your grandpa got a good job as a roofer, and then he became the foreman. We bought a large white house and had enough money to start collecting antiques. It was the kind of house that could occupy your grandfather for years. He built a porch deck, patio furniture, and corner shelves. He got me a white statue of La Virgen de Guadalupe to put near the circular driveway. You painted it for me one summer, do you remember? We had a lot of land for his work shed and my garden and berry trees. He built me a china cabinet for my Mexican dishes. He built a two-car garage and a woodworking area. He was always doing something; he's never been able to sit still.

WWII was basically over the year after we got married. Your grandpa tried to enlist as a volunteer, but they didn't want him because he was a Mexican citizen. He had moved back here to the U.S. when he was five years old and was legal, but he hadn't been naturalized. Ama Lolita, your grandpa's mother, moved her family to Mexico so her oldest son, Francisco, would not be drafted into WWI—they took them real young back then. Your great-grandmother was born in what is now Laredo, Texas long before Texas became part of the union. She only moved to Mexico for that short period to keep her son out of the war, and that is where your grandpa was born.

Your grandfather and I talked about it once, how good our childhoods were. We were poor, yes, but we don't ever remember being hungry. It wasn't until we were older and had gotten married that we were a little hungry because they were rationing the food during the war. Even then, I would take that food and make some nice little caldos. This is when women started working in factories. It was also when we used to get tickets for shoes. I never wore out my shoes so I would give my ticket to my sister Lupe who would always wear out one side of her shoes. She was always getting into things, climbing trees and things. I practically raised her and was not going to have her looking raggedy, so I always gave her my ticket for a new pair of shoes.

Your grandpa's grandparents were both Spanish and one of his great grandparents on his dad's side was French. My great grandfather was from Spain, his last name was Montemayor—which means big forest. The Spanish on my side comes from my mother, your great-grandmother. It was my grandfather who had Indian from his mother in Mexico and Spanish from his father. My great-great-grandma on my dad's side, the Sosa's— was Indian but her husband was Spanish. My mom's dad was from Mexico and his parents were from Mexico, even though he was born in Corpus. My mom's mom's side was Spanish—her sisters have red hair and my mom had red hair too with green eyes and freckles. Your mom has this down in one of those trees of the whole family. I think only you and her are interested in these things. I think your mom even traced someone on your grandfather's side back to Portugal; it may be the French one. It's good to know where you come from, even though we are Mexican, that's what we are. It's just like now, all the kids are falling in love with other kinds of people, it wasn't like it used to be. All my new grandchildren are Mexican American, but you know, we have German, Polish, and African. And then we have just plain old white. It doesn't really matter. We are all mixed up now. It's the way the world is changing, and it can only be a good thing that people realize we are not so much different as we think we are.

On August 29, 2019, my grandmother Emilia, who is 91 years old, will pass away. It's been a steady decline and throughout this period, I will dream of her and visit her in my sleep. I can feel her in the "in-between," space as I go about my working day. And then the day she's been waiting for forever since her husband, my grandfather, passed away will come. She will be gone from this earth, and my memories will thread backward in time to millions of delicate moments in my childhood when I understood who I was in the world because of her.

20.

The useless, the odd, the peculiar, the incongruous—are signs of history. They supply proof that the world was not made in its present form. When history perfects, it covers its own tracks.

Stephen Jay Gould, *The Panda's Thumb*

July 2006. I have lost my English words. Four hours of Spanish a day in the sweltering Mayan heat, and I forget language because I'm knee-deep in the presente progresivo del subjuntivo. Juan Carlos speaks English, French, and Spanish and is currently learning German. He changes languages when he changes girlfriends. I'm not allowed my English, and eventually, it starts to fade away while my brain fills up with irregular verbs. There is a total of twenty-one irregular verbs in Spanish, which, according to Juan Carlos, makes Spanish an easy language to learn. I would not have imagined that learning the difference between "have," "had," "would have," and "will have had," could throw me into such discord. But there you have it, the difference between a fluent Spanish language speaker and the rest of the people. He asks me what I want out of class, and I say, "to travel anywhere in Latin or South America." He says that I can do that already and get food, shelter, and all the necessities of life, and perhaps make a few friends. "What else," he asks. I want to know Spanish so well I dream in it. I want to understand completely the Spanish side of Pablo Neruda's pages. I want to carry on an entire conversation with my grandfather. Those are good answers, he says, as I deliver them in the nightmare of the presente perfecto.

C and I rent a car in Playa del Carmen and drive to Tulum (which means "walled" in Mayan), which is the state of my heart. Run, I tell myself. We return to Casa Magna after dinner late one evening, the yoga instructor from Los Angeles, the Bolivian receptionist, the Chinese American dude from Phoenix, and the groundskeeper are all on bended knees watching two Mexican biologists excavate the last of 173 eggs being laid by the largest and only sea turtle I've ever seen. It's completely dark save for the headlamps strapped to the biologists' heads. It would be a miracle to watch this if it were not for the concerted biological strategy underway to make sure turtle eggs reach maturation. All sea turtle species are considered endangered or threatened. The biologists describe the size in meters, so I have no idea how big this turtle really is, and I am too embarrassed to ask them to calculate it in feet. I try to compare it to the length and width of my large coffee table, but that doesn't seem fantastic enough.

I wonder where she's come from, this turtle. She has dug herself a hole in the sand the size of a semi-truck tire and is currently laying her eggs, only to cover them completely while digging herself out of the hole and making her way back to the sea. Adult female sea turtles return to the beach where they were born to lay their eggs in the sand. When the baby turtles hatch, they immediately head for nearby water and it's during this difficult trip that predators eat the baby turtles. It has been estimated that only 1% of these hatchlings will reach adulthood. In the morning, what look like tire tracks on the beach are the only evidence the mama turtle has left behind. In all likelihood, she will come back in fifteen days and lay 200 more eggs in exactly the same spot she did this evening, and again next year, and the year after that, and the year after that. I feel like this mama turtle where year after year, I return to the same spot, trying to dig myself out of a larger and larger hole.

I learn that the tortoise represents longevity, one of the five most sought-after values in Chinese culture: luck, prosperity, double happiness, and wealth are the others. Longevity is the most highly esteemed. The crane is also a symbol of longevity. So are the pine tree, the cypress, bamboo, and longevity peaches, which aren't really peaches at all; they are buns made to look like peaches and filled with red bean, date, or lotus-seed paste. Longevity sounds like long and levity, and I wonder if there is any connection between those two words.

Could levity make you live a long life? Should I lighten up?

Vivien Sung, in *Five-Fold Happiness,* describes the God of Longevity as the most popular of the stellar gods, outshining the God of Luck and the God of Prosperity. His name, Shou, literally means "longevity star." The God is a benevolent old gentleman with a smiling face and a prominent forehead who holds a dragon-headed walking stick in one hand and the peach of immortality in the other.

The legend, as Sung describes it, is about a nineteen-year-old boy named Yan Chao who meets a sage and learns that he is destined to die the next day. The boy pleads for his life as do his parents, but the sage tells them it is not within his power to change fate. The sage instructs the parents to prepare a meal of venison and wine for their son to deliver to two men who will be sitting under a mulberry tree playing chess. He warns Yan Chao not to say a word under any circumstances. The following day, Yan Chao provides the men with their meal, but they are so engrossed in a game of chess that they do not notice who has delivered it. A few games later, they notice Yan Chao and realize they are eating all his offerings. They decide to repay his generosity by altering the Register of Destiny.

The man to the north says it will not be an easy task. The man to the south, on inspecting the Register more closely, believes it can be modified easily. He takes out a brush and changes nineteen years to ninety-one years. Yan Chao returns home and lives to the ripe old age of ninety-one.

In my legend, I cook a far superlative meal for two female Gods who notice immediately the offering I've made for them and therefore, do not keep me waiting. In my Register of Destiny, they both come across Virginia and concur that her premature death was a severe oversight. Fate had nothing to do with it. It was a simple mistake, and they will reason that it makes no sense to have robbed the world of such beauty and love. While one goddess is busy licking her fingers, the other goddess easily rectifies the situation by writing upon the stars that nine years is supposed to be ninety-nine. This sits well with me. She will outlive all of us and we won't have to be the ones living without her.

21.

I was there, so it seems to me that I should be able to remember everything. But, no, I don't remember very much...except the feeling.

Peggy Rodriguez-TenEyck

In the Spring of 2008, I'm thinking of this idea of "living a long time" while I sit in the UCLA Olive View Medical Center. I have no health insurance, and I'm bleeding too much. It's a perfect metaphor, really. I'm convinced that my body is responding to stress. In the waiting room, my thoughts compete with the Jerry Springer show. I've learned a lot about the California state health care system for people like me. I've learned, more importantly, that if there had been something seriously wrong with me, I could've died before my next scheduled appointment five months from now, wherein the doctors would perform one more test to rule out one more possible diagnosis. My name is called and pronounced correctly in Spanish by the Iranian nurse, who is surprised to see someone who looks like me, in a place like that. I'm wearing flip-flops and expensive jeans and have two post-graduate degrees, but I can't afford health insurance. Something may be wrong with me, but I look pretty good.

I've "earned a biopsy," says the resident. Months later I will have a sonogram and months after that I will have a sonohistogram or a histosonogram or something...the first test is inconclusive. I've been told to drink as much water as possible before my appointment, and now I really have to pee. I sit in the waiting room watching Oprah, wishing I could do something worthy of her discovering me so that I could be rich, and then I could afford insurance and not have to sit in this dingy waiting room watching her on television. I'm suddenly feeling very alone and very sick. My mouth goes watery, and my head goes hot. I go to the restroom in the entryway, but it's occupied. I'm not going to make it. I curl up in the corner, praying no one walks into the hallway while I vomit up my water.

By this time, I'm in tears. I can't help myself. I tell the nurse behind the desk that I'm so very sorry, but I've gotten sick in the hallway. She does not seem the least bit concerned. Perhaps I don't look sick. I finally get into the bathroom, and someone has been in here smoking. I take a handful of paper towels and clean up my own mess before anyone notices. The secret doors at the end of the hallway open, but no one comes in and no one goes out. I think of making a run for it when my name is called. The pictures are not good. I was supposed to be full of water. I tried to explain that I was full of water, but I puked in the hallway and then I was so distracted that I forgot and peed. No one cares about my sob story, not even me. However sick I feel it cannot compare to the loneliness of this experience and the degree of self-pity that will shroud my already debilitating mood.

No one can tell me why I'm having two periods a month, only that it is causing me to be anemic. I decide to handle this on my own or rather my friend Jane handles it for me and pays for me to see her holistic doctor who gives me herbs instead of pills. Three months later, all is well—at least physically.

Two years earlier in May of 2006, Jane insists on taking all the luggage out of the car, which is considerable in my opinion. She is going to live in Berkeley for two months, and it's really fucking hot in Buttonwillow. She wins. She's cunning. Before I can protest a moment longer, she has graciously asked a nice Indian man who is now going up the stairs with the two heaviest pieces of luggage. I'm removed of the opportunity to be the strong, agile, can-doer. It gives me pleasure to be strong for Jane. It lifts me up to lift her up in a one-arm hug, so her feet dangle and her spine re-aligns itself. The air is thick with loss because her heart is broken, and she is on the perilous road back to sanity. We discuss this a lot, of course. It's not that she was happy. It's that now she's alone and that's worse. I nod when she reminds me that she was born prematurely and that must have something to do with it. We fill her royal blue Mini Cooper with music that I've picked especially for this road trip.

Nina Simone can make you glad you know what sorrow is.

It seems odd to me that we stop driving when there are plenty more hours of daylight. But here we are, lying on two double beds in an ugly but oddly comforting room. We watch a news special on the history of the AIDS epidemic, which has the effect of a car crash—it's horrifying, and we feel grateful for our health and the distraction, however serious it is, but we can't take our eyes off it.

I will attempt to help make Jane's exterior life as complete and organized as possible. I will attempt to help her construct a home away from home as if it will transform her on the inside. There is so much to do because there is so little to say. I get to be the boss, really, and I'm slightly embarrassed by how much I enjoy it. I suggest we stop at the Berkeley Bowl as soon as we are in town. We drive down Shattuck and buy a futon on the spot, just in time for Jacqi to show up and help us haul it to Jane's temporary new house in the Berkeley hills, henceforth called Northgate. It's idyllic really, a terraced landscape with deer and bunnies, and a spectacular view of the bay. I insist that she let me take her to Ikea for a cheap desk, which I put together. I also put together her Copenhagen bed frame. We shop for a flat-screen television. I take pride in getting shit done because I feel woefully inadequate at helping her heal her heart. We take walks through pine and juniper while trying to guess what people have paid for houses way up here. We get lost, but it doesn't matter because this is the "lost and found" trip. Jane will write *Midnights* because that is what writers do, they write, regardless of their mood. When interviewed about the book Jane said, "Well, yes, landscape is important to me, in this book, but I would quickly add that, while many of these pieces take place in the American West, it is the landscape of the heart that is my subject, my story; place is foreground, and background, to the story of heartache; this is, in effect, my confession."

Jane will receive a call in the middle of the night about her mother Florence, who lives in Florida, and in the morning, I will take her to the airport.

Months later when we are back at Jane's permanent home in Tucson, she will read something from her book *Midnights*. "It is always midnight inhabiting a strange place," which she wrote in an essay of the same title but a different project. I read the essay late at night when Jane is sleeping. I can smell creosote, and Jane's peacock enters my dreams:

> Wherever the traveler goes in a quest for beauty and knowledge, if the place responds like a peacock displaying its iridescence, we have the stuff legends are made of. Imagery explodes and creates a derangement of the senses. Those who have already gone and returned no longer remember it that way, or remember the place fondly, or inexactly. But during the ritual visit itself, the unfamiliar and disoriented prevail, requiring that we notice things in their entirety, which we must do to "get anywhere" in the confrontation with the new. To see a thing entire is to see its otherworldliness, to see the stripes and the fangs and the sausage-like intestines, working the analogical possibilities to experience it ("it" is, by now, a monstrous thing).

I think she speaks of Greece, and because I am going through a selfish period where everything reminds me of my own life, she speaks of me. Everything is new, and to get anywhere I must notice things in their entirety. The ritual visits to myself, where the unfamiliar and disoriented prevail. I am by now, a monstrous thing. But I am ill-equipped to describe what I experience, and while peacocks escape from her fingers, I flutter around simply trying to get down on paper, words like hard, sadness, and you. I miss Kim. She is a Southern girl who has it in her genes to be spirited. The usual visits to Jane and Kim's home always included the spreading out of delicious food and drink and funny conversation like today was our last day on earth, and we were too beautiful for mediocrity. When in the company of an aesthete, the world turns to peacocks and champagne. It's been a long summer. It's been a long life so far.

Jane will lose Kim. I will lose C. For some time, we'll both be in the pool trying to swim off the grief. I knew then it was never about her—so my curiosity continued. One day, Jane will demand that I (we) get over it and that enough is enough, and I'm (we're) done learning whatever the breakup was supposed to teach me (us). I finally hear her, and we agree.

22.

How does a part of this world leave the world? How does wetness leave water?

Rumi

One summer, my sister and I are riding in the back of my Tía Maggie and Tío Manuel's dark green station wagon, the one with the wood paneling on the side. Peggy is the oldest and so she gets to sit in the front. My Tía Maggie sits in the middle, her long legs stretched out and her bare feet on the dash. She is pulling her leg hairs out with a tweezer, one by one. I'm concerned she won't finish the job by the time we get to Texas, but no one else is. Jo-Jo, Eddie-boy, and I are sitting in the back seat, and Gina, Connie, and Israel are stuck in the furthest back with all the groceries and luggage, because they are the smallest and they are too young to mind. Pre-seatbelt era. We stop at a gas station in the middle of nowhere and climb out in time for us not to pull each other's hair out. It's peanut butter and jelly or bologna and cheese on Wonder Bread. I've never liked cold cuts, so I choose peanut butter. I want to spread my own peanut butter, but Tía says everyone is going to get what she makes and that's final. We bow our heads and devour our sandwiches on the curb with our Mountain Dews and watch the semi-trucks rolling in and rolling out of the gas station. It's hot and humid and, for some reason, my uncle is always looking under the hood of the car every time we stop for gas. We frantically pull the imaginary horn above our heads to get the semi-trucks to respond and honk. Peggy watches us with a curiosity that is difficult to imagine if you're not a teenager. Jo-Jo lets out a fart, something he has done and will continue to do with pride and amusement our entire childhoods. Then we are stuffed back into the car, climbing over things, stretching out the towel so we don't scald the back of our legs on the vinyl.

When we are older, Peggy and I will have our picture taken wearing Chicano Power T-shirts in my grandmother's backyard. They are bright yellow with black felt letters. I don't know what Chicano means since it's mostly a California thing and we are growing up in Ohio, but I'm supposed to be proud to wear it so I am. Peggy will have a quinceñera on her 15th birthday, as will I. We will spend our summers swimming. We will listen to the John Mellencamp album in her bedroom when he was still John Cougar. She will marry her high school sweetheart and eventually she will have four kids of her own, the oldest of which will become the mother of three girls, two of them twins.

Peggy is no longer in shock. But to this day, the smallest memories can bring tears to her beautiful hazel eyes. She stands in the yard waiting for me to walk back towards the house after my mother has told me that my sister and cousin have died. She is holding her mouth, weeping, hugs me tightly, and then walks me back inside the house: two older sisters without our sisters.

Memoria of Peggy Rodriguez-TenEyck

My day was okay I guess, I was just getting ready for the slumber party at Rachel's house for her 8th birthday, and Patty and I were going to be chaperoning. I remember it being a nice and beautiful day, warm and sunny. My dad was going to band practice at Rachel's house that night as well because Rachel's dad was also in the band. He would always go to work after band practice because he worked the 11 pm-7 am shift at that time. Pattie and I were in the front of my dad's old model truck, and Connie and Gina were sitting in the back. We were on our way when for some reason we had to turn back, my dad had to have forgotten something. I remember the girls playing in the back because Connie burned herself on the smoke-stack-looking pipe that stuck out of the side of the truck. It was by the driver's side. My mom looked at it and kissed it and told Connie she would be fine. So, we started off again. I remember my mom waving goodbye as we were leaving. Pattie and I were talking about the party and what we would do to make it fun for all the younger girls when all of sudden my dad tries to swerve to the right in order to miss the car that was going to hit us on the left side, and once he swerved, we went through the field and flipped over, I think a couple of times. We landed on all four tires because I remember being able to get out once the truck stopped. I got out of the truck with only one shoe on, for some reason, this has stayed with me, the fact about my shoe.

I followed Pattie, but I think I felt like I was by myself. I remember crying and screaming for my dad, but I couldn't find him. Then I started calling for my mom, "Mom where are you"? I just kept spinning and spinning. I really didn't understand what was happening to me. I saw someone lying on the road, but I couldn't tell who it was, so I ran over there and saw that it was Connie on her belly.

All I could see was her back and the side of her head and her shoulder blade, I think. Once I found her, I couldn't see anyone else. The next thing I remember was my dad flipping out, going back and forth. He went after the lady, I think. He was so upset and confused that I think he wanted to hurt her. The next thing I remember was that they put Pattie and me in a police car, and I remember looking out and not seeing anyone. All I could do was scream for my mom. I was so scared, and afraid. I don't remember seeing Pattie from the time I got out of the truck, till I don't know when. The next thing I remember I was sitting in a chair at the hospital, and just watching all the adults crying and hugging each other, but I couldn't hear them. It was like I was on the outside looking in, and I was watching my own bad dream.

Until this day I can't remember what anyone was saying. I think it's very strange that I can't remember hearing anyone, and that I don't remember anyone coming to me. It makes me so upset that I don't even remember anything from the funeral home. Just that it was a closed casket for both, but maybe not. There are just bits and pieces, and so much of the story is missing. I feel sad about that. I was there, so it seems to me that I should be able to remember everything. But, no, I don't remember very much... except the feeling, which is next to impossible to describe. I was fourteen years old, a freshman at Eisenhower Junior High School. Now, I'm a mother of four and a grandmother, and I can't even fathom what our parents have gone through in losing a child. How does one recover from something like that? How do you keep going? But we all did, didn't we?

23.

The castle of the emotional mind is not yet grounded in fact, and there is ample room left within its domain for conjecture, invention, and poetry.

Thomas Lewis, M.D., Fari Amini, M.D., Richard Lannon, M.D.: *A General Theory of Love*

Five months after my sister's death, on October 31st, 1978, it's her birthday. My mom and I stay in and watch movies. We had gone to K-Mart to purchase Halloween candy in case any kids stopped by. Since I no longer felt like a kid, I no longer felt like I was missing anything, and with a stroke of luck, my desire for candy had disappeared. When my sister was alive, her birthday parties consisted of everyone wearing their Halloween costumes. She was always a princess, and I was always a hobo. If you live in a frugal family, you get to be a princess or a hobo. One must commit fully to being someone else in order to do Halloween. I'm not the only one who feels this way. Weston could not commit to being a cowboy one year and cried in the backyard because his mustache was not working. Granted, he was six years old, but "el punto aqui es" (as my friend Wendy would say) Halloween should be left to the fully committed. I must outthink my stubborn and recalcitrant heart if I'm going to attempt another Halloween.

There were other things I could no longer do after Gina died. For example, I could not do math. I was never strong at math, which would explain why I was always trying to impress myself by using it, but after her death, I was worse. I'm sitting at my desk in Mrs. Murphy's 4th-grade class when the quiz begins. Mrs. Murphy wore cat-eye glasses, which hung on a delicate silver chain, and skirts in grey, dark green, dark blue, and brown with cardigans in all the same colors, but she never wore the same colors together, it was always grey skirt with a brown cardigan or dark green skirt with a grey cardigan. She had big hands and wore comfortable black or brown shoes.

The quiz happens every Friday, and I'm required to do a full page of multiplication problems. My first Friday back at school, I stare at the page full of numbers and they look like Chinese characters to me. I dig the pencil into my middle finger, where I've developed a pencil callous. My feet are moving furiously over one another, and my heart is beating fast. I'm going to fail. I know it. I have done this a million times before, one day a week all year long. I've even earned some stars on my chart. I don't have an owl, but my best friend Melinda Dobrosky has one and I'm very proud of her for that. There is a large white chart with our names written in a column on the back wall of the classroom. We started with colored stars, moved to silver stars, and then to gold. After the stars, one could earn smiley faces, and then the ultimate, the owl. Later, I will think of Connie's owls and then amuse myself with the bouncy nature of all thoughts as they ping pong off my brain. I can't do the quiz and it terrifies me. I'm almost in tears when I take my quiz to the back of the room where Mrs. Murphy is busy doing teacherly things and whisper in my own surprise, "I can't do my times-tables," as if I were saying, "I can't tie my shoelaces." She nods her head without looking up at me and holds out her hand for me to give her the paper I'm clutching, my failure. She says nothing. I'm waiting for her to look at me, to ask me what the problem is. "They're just numbers," she always says, but this time she nods smiling, and keeps about her busyness. When I'm convinced that she is not going to say anything, I turn around and go back to my seat, trying not to cry. She never mentioned it. I didn't get a grade. She didn't say, "Sorry your sister is dead, sweetheart." She just let my quiz slip by as if I never took it, it never happened. They're just numbers after all. I loved her after that day.

I am fifteen years old and spending the night at my cousin Rachel's house. We decide to go to the video store to rent a comedy, or a drama, and we sneakily select a porn movie from the curtained room in the back of the video store. We are trying not to laugh at the titles, but some are so outrageous that our eyes bug out. We settle on *Charlie's Angels*, which seemed the most subdued and did not have boobs and things broadcasting the cover as a porn movie. We escape from the store as quickly as possible, hoping the cashier would allow us to rent the movie. He doesn't even flinch. When we get home, Tía Eva wants to see what we picked, in case she wants to join us. My heart stops. Knowing her mother and having rightfully predicted this, Rachel had shoved the porn movie into her purse, away from the other films. We save it for last just in case my Tía Eva is inspired to come in and hang out with the girls for movie night.

We watch the different angels getting banged in the office by a business executive, in the kitchen by a chef, in the garage by a mechanic, and on a yacht by a sailor. We don't say anything as the quilts are shielding us from seeing each other. The volume is so low it's practically on mute when one of the angels cries out, "Oh Charlie, Charlie!" I look up at Rachel, and we both bust out in a fit of laughter.

Memoria of Rachel Salas

As I sit here writing, I can feel my throat tightening and my eyes filling up even though it was so long ago. I was only eight years old. It was May 19, 1978, and I was waiting for you, Connie and Gina to arrive along with Peggy and Tía Patty, who were chaperoning my birthday pajama party. Connie and Gina were my favorite cousins, and we were very close. You would always see them, one on each side of me in just about all the photos I have of my childhood. I remember waiting for a very long time for them to arrive, and I kept asking what was taking them so long. I overheard my mom whisper to my dad that they should've arrived already. I then heard them on the phone constantly, calling different people until my dad and the other guys went looking for them, it made me nervous. All I remember is them coming back saying that there had been an accident. I was sitting outside on the porch when I was told, but I cannot recall how they told me the girls had died. I don't remember what they said. I can only remember the feeling of knowing, and then I began crying. All the friends who had arrived for my party had to go home.

It is especially difficult for me around the time of my birthday, since that's when it all happened. I remember after the girls died, I would ask God, why them? I would pray every night for them to come back to me because I needed them. And then I would ask God to just bring them to me in my dreams. No matter how much I thought of them, I never saw them in my dreams. I really didn't understand anything, but as I got older and my faith became stronger, I believed that God needed them to be our angels; at least that is what I told myself. I have bits and pieces of memories; some are vivid, and others are distant and hazy.

I can't remember the days after I found out. I barely remember the funeral, except that I was in my communion dress, standing in the front of their caskets. I don't know if I stood there crying over the loss of them, or if I was just in shock, and since I was only eight years old, I didn't really know what to do with all of it. What do you know about death at that age? Somehow, I understood that I was never going to see them, talk to them or play with them, ever again and that was overwhelming.

I feel grateful for the memories that have endured over time. Every time I was with Connie, we would play "house" with our pretend boyfriends or husbands, or hide-and-seek, or kickball, or ride bikes. I really wish that my memories were clearer. As for Gina, there was this one time we were playing house and she pretended her husband was Troy Anderson (the son of the seventh-grade math teacher). I remember her getting upset with him, and she told him that she was leaving him and pretended to pack her things. She went to the closet and told him that he would have to take care of the kids; I laugh at that now. We were so silly. She was crazy about him, and he may have been her boyfriend at the time of the accident. I do remember seeing him at the funeral with his parents.

I remember staying the weekends in Reno with you guys and taking walks down by Lake Erie. We used to climb the rocks to get to the beach area and go swimming. In the winter we would all go ice-skating. Over the years I heard about all the events that surrounded the death of the girls. Things I knew nothing about for a long time, and each time I would find out something strange and new, it struck the very core of me all over again. And to think we easily could have lost you. I am so glad that after the girls died, you and I started spending a lot of time together. I would stay the night with you on the weekends. I think that might have been something that we both needed to help fill the void, and as a result, we developed a closeness, which I am very thankful for. I wish my memories of them are as solid as the ones I have of you, but I suppose, as you get older it's easier to remember.

I often wonder what kinds of things the girls and I would've done together. Would I have gotten as close to you if they had been around? Maybe I wouldn't have gone to your college classes or taken that stupid picture of us with Poncho the Donkey when we were in Mexico or ridden up the mountain on your motorcycle when you lived in Arizona, and sunbathed on a huge rock by a waterfall, and then came across a rattlesnake on our way back down. I still have a scar from your motorcycle. In fact, we both have the same scar on our calves from that muffler. That scar is a lasting memory. That scar is a good scar.

24.

Laughter, whether conciliatory or terrible, always occurs when some fear passes. It indicates liberation either from danger or from the grip of logic.

Theodor Adorno, *Dialectic of Enlightenment*

June 2011. Body parts wear down and then they wear out. My people are getting old, and one day they will be gone. My grandfather Gilbrando is getting his other knee replaced at Christus Hospital in Kingsville, Texas. Spending the remainder of his life unable to play golf is not acceptable. I'm spending the remainder of the night in a baby blue room next to the chapel reserved for families who do that sort of thing. There is a floor lamp that casts the kind of warm light one wants in their bedroom, and a glass jar filled with travel-size soaps and shampoos. The nun, Sister Elizabeth arranged the room for my grandmother so she could take her naps there without having to go back to the Quality Inn. Sister Elizabeth calls my grandfather "brother" in her thick Irish brogue. "What's this, brother, you must eat to get well," the sister says. I, of course, completely disagree with this philosophy and when she leaves, I whisper to my grandfather that he doesn't have to eat any of this crap, "Just drink the liquids," I say, as I hand him a cup with a large straw that bends at the end.

In the lobby area is a wall dedicated to the pictures of the soldiers from Kingsville, Texas, who are serving in Iraq. Soon, after more than seven years of war, 4,400 U.S. casualties, and tens of thousands of Iraqi civilians killed, the United States will officially end its combat mission in Iraq. I spend a lot of time looking at them while the nurses do things that require us to leave my grandfather's room. My grandmother Emilia insists on hanging up his clothes in the hospital closet, so they aren't wrinkled when he gets to leave. I situate her on a large reclining chair where she will sit watching her husband of sixty-plus years recuperate and suggest things we can do for him since she can't do them herself because she has Parkinson's. My aunts and I are her arms and legs.

The following night I sit in a reclining chair with my grandfather until midnight, watching a nature show on hippos in Spanish, and then head to my blue room. I imagine them taking me in the middle of the night for some operation I don't need because they mixed up the rooms until I notice that this room can be locked from the inside. I lock it. I wash up, put on my pajamas, and climb on top of my enormous electric bed. I push a large button to adjust the firmness and another button so I can sit up and another button to elevate my legs. It's not a sacrifice to be here. In fact, I'm happy I don't have to listen to my Tía Eva snore as she falls asleep. In the morning I will go to his room, and he will be waiting with his small leather toiletry bag sitting in front of him on one of those hospital tables. I open the bag and pull out his shaving cream, his razor, and his Old Spice aftershave. I fill up a cup of water. He applies the shaving cream to his face, and I realize I have to get a washcloth for him to wipe his hand. I apply a little hair tonic, Vitalis, to his head and brush back his hair. I'm amazed that although he is going bald on the top of his head, he nonetheless, at the age of eighty-three, has mostly black hair. The same is true for my grandmother. She says that they both joked because they were looking forward to their hair turning white, but it hasn't happened. I apply paste to his toothbrush, and he brushes for a good long time. I realize I need a cup for him to spit it out and another cup full of water so he can rinse. I'm new at this. He insists on applying deodorant even though he doesn't smell, and he's not going anywhere. There. He's ready to accept a full day's worth of phone calls.

In the evening, my Tías, Eva, and Maggie stay at the hospital with my grandfather while I take my grandmother back to the hotel and give her a long massage with lavender oil and Tiger Balm. The massage I gave her last night helped her sleep through the night, until 4:45 a.m., for the first time in a very long time, so I decide to give her a massage every night I'm here. "You're a Godsend, Mija," she says. I'm surprised how much there is to do. We shuttle my grandmother back and forth, go to Walmart to exchange my grandfather's watch, get him a mirror for shaving, get back in time to go get my grandmother's lunch, go get flowers for the nurses and Sister Elisabeth, and thank you cards for everyone else. I make phone calls to arrange the delivery of his knee machine.

On the last night of my grandfather's stay, I drive my grandmother home. She has me arrange things for his return. She calls him twice while they are both watching the same telenovela, *Querida Enemiga*. My Tía Maggie will have cleaned the entire house. I go for a run and take notice of the rolling hills, the cows, and pastures. I turn off my iPod and listen to the humming bugs and birds. When I return to the house, I make a salad with avocado instead of eating ten flour tortillas. I invite my Tías to eat salad with me. "You only have one body," I tell them. Bodies are fragile and amazingly resilient, tissues and water mixed with spirit and fortitude. After one of my health lectures, my Tío Manuel says, "Mija, we're all going to die." "That's not the problem," I say, "the problem is living while you're sick." I've decided that won't be me. I want to die healthy, preferably in a natural disaster.

In the morning I drive back to Kingsville with my Tío Gil, and we will pick up my grandfather and take him home. I know he's feeling better once he has successfully, albeit painfully, got into the front seat of the car because, on our way out of the driveway of the hospital, he criticizes my driving. He accuses me of being like my Tía Maggie who waits too long instead of pulling out when you have the chance. He then tells me I'm going 40mph in a 30mph zone and that I did not come to a complete and final stop at that intersection, the one in the middle of nowhere with no cars in sight. Later that night, he calls me into his room and tells me how much he appreciates me, "Te quiero, te quiero mucho," he says as he pats my face like he's always done my whole life. A familiar knot wells up in my throat, and I have to walk outside and take a deep breath.

He and my grandmother Emilia welcome death at any moment. They live every day understanding that the end of their life is near, and they are completely at peace with this fact. It's the rest of us who have issues.

25.

The objective world simply is; it does not happen. Only to the gaze of my consciousness, crawling upward along the lifeline of my body, does a section of this world come to life as a fleeting image which continuously changes in time.

Herman Weyl, Mathematical Physicist

In April of 2003, Weston and I go to the Getty to spend some time in the garden. It's my hope that he will be amenable to seeing the exhibit "The Passions" by Bill Viola. It's a perfect day. This eight-year-old genius marvels that, "We don't really have to go into the buildings to see the art because we are standing in the art." We read that the stones they used to build the Getty are Travertine, the same stones they used to build the Roman Coliseum and other Roman wonders. He likes this fact. He is a connoisseur of facts. He loves them as much as he loves frozen raspberries and coffee ice cream.

Emotions are the point—extravagant emotions such as joy, sorrow, fear, and wonder are what we experience together in the biblical tableaus that are projected on variously sized plasma screens. For example, "The Quintet of the Astonished," commissioned by the National Gallery, London, was inspired by Hieronymus Bosch's painting of a quartet of executioners surrounding Christ, called "Etonnement avec Frayeur (Astonishment Mixed with Fright)," after Charles Le Brun (French, 1619-1690). The expressions change ever so slowly, but nonetheless dramatically over time, such that you feel like you are the only person witnessing the pictures revealing themselves, finally free of the still-life. Weston looks back at me, eyes wide in amazement, and says, "The paintings are moving." They are. Everyone's expressions in the video paintings are moving, barely, extremely slowly. One of my favorites is "Catherine's Room" (2001), which was inspired by "Saint Catherine of Siena Praying," about 1393-94, by Andrea de Bartolo (Italian, 1358/64-1428). Viola adapted the form of the predella to convey scenes of a daily life touched with sanctity.

The films have been shot on 70mm (the epic format reserved for films like *Lawrence of Arabia*) and then projected on various sized plasma screens. The effect is mystical. If the substance or subjects of paintings could move, this is how they would do it. I read that Viola is fascinated by Christian ascetics and Buddhist hermits, whose renunciation of companionship and comfort makes possible a life of pure devotion. In his notebook, he wrote, "Make a piece for nuns...for the woman who takes comfort in herself, who finds companionship in an empty room." I think of Saint Teresa preferring solitude and the company of God to everyone else. And I think to myself that I may want to put a little more effort into this notion of comfort and figure out where to get some. Right now, I'm comfortable with Weston, and I'm comfortable with Viola. We make our way to an enormous side installation, a little apart from the rest (well-designed, I think), and we sit on pews. It's good to sit because looking at a video painting by Bill Viola clearly takes some time. We watch the "Last Supper" happening before our eyes. Extreme slow motion reveals the minute shifts and complexity of feelings. I agree with Weston, when he whispers, "You can really see things when they move slow."

February 2008, Texas. It's 2:24 a.m. and I can't sleep. The clock that sits on the shelf inside the headboard is ticking loudly. I manage to take out the batteries in the dark. I look over at my grandmother, Ama Mela, who is now and may forever continue sleeping on her dead husband's twin bed. I'm very hot and so I move to the other side of my grandmother's bed and open the window. I move myself so I can feel the Texas breeze on my face. Opening the window creates a small symphony of other distractions. There is a dog barking in the distance, and now I notice how bright the light is coming from my Tía Janey's double-wide, which sits at an odd angle in front of my grandparents' house. The door creaks open, then closes, creaks open, then closes. The light blue plastic blinds now swing in and out, bumping into the edge of the window. I get up in the dark and squeeze the clean white cotton socks that are sitting on the dresser under the door, so it doesn't move. I take the small piece of cloth that has been nailed to the side of the window and anchor the blinds to a small nail, so they don't move. I imagine Apa Chele having rigged it for exactly this purpose. I am wide-awake. I listen to the low hum of the nighttime chorus outside my window—the dog barks, the bugs sing, the door creeks, the blinds quiver. I resign myself to the light since it's out of my control, but otherwise, try and exert my influence on everything else that is creating sound. The whole experience begs to be a country song. A Latin hip-hop bass guitar thudding loudly on the street outside my Los Angeles apartment will not seem as loud to me as this cacophony of Texas crickets.

I finally lie comfortably back in bed and look out the window; I notice the neighbor's house across the road, the one who picked me off the ground; their red and blue Christmas lights twinkling in springtime. I look over at my grandmother and notice she has one outstretched arm hanging over the bed. A strange sensation comes over me, like a pure certainty or understanding. I've woken up numerous times and the first thing I see is my arm in exactly the same position, stretched out beyond the bed, dangling in mid-air. I can't recall the last time I was this present, and I can't recall what time it is when I finally fall asleep in my dead grandfather's room in the middle of the night in the middle of nowhere, more at peace than I can remember feeling in a long while.

Apa Chele was the first to wake up in the morning. In the winter, he would start the furnace and space heaters, go to the kitchen, and make Ama Mela her "butter toast," white bread toasted with margarine and some strawberry jam cut into four pieces with a cup of coffee. He would bring it to her bedside and lay out her medications so she could take them as soon as she had something in her stomach. He'd climb back into bed and wait for her. The bedroom is big enough for a double bed where my grandmother slept and a single bed where my grandfather slept, a television, vanity dresser, and small nightstand in between the beds. The sheets are clean, crisp, and very old, mismatched with patterns of flowers, stripes, and solids. You can see the box spring patterned in black with fuchsia-colored flowers. Several different-sized blankets are layered on top of the sheets. On the morning of my grandfather's funeral, it's my father who comes in with my grandmother's butter toast. I stretch myself to wake up and help my grandmother get dressed. I pull her sheer black stockings over her permanently swollen feet. She holds up her nightgown as I slip her capri pants up to her waist and try to fasten the top button. She sucks in a little giggling until I manage. "Don't laugh today, or your button will pop," I say. She laughs. She pulls off her gown and her large breasts melt into her stomach. She shows me the scar where she had triple bypass surgery, explaining why she can't wear a bra anymore. When my Tía Janey arrives, she is relieved that my grandmother is already dressed.

We will bury my grandfather at the new Collins Cemetery. My cousins will release a small group of doves after my cousin Cesar cries his way through delivering a poem. We will go back to el rancho and have barbecued chicken. I will eat fruit cups with chili powder and all the men will congregate around a fire in the backyard. All the women will stay inside the house with my grandmother and talk about old stories, old memories, and old times. That night, the night before I leave Texas, four of us granddaughters are in the bedroom listening to my grandmother talk about her late husband. Jeanette, my cousin who is a nurse explains to my grandmother the difference between her heart condition and my grandfather's heart condition because Ama Mela is seriously confused about how she could not have known her husband was not feeling well. This is her puzzle. Jeanette delicately explains in perfect Spanish that Ama Mela's condition is caused by a clot outside her heart and so when the blood flow to her heart gets restricted, she can feel the pain directly in her chest. My grandfather's condition, in contrast, originated inside his heart and restricted the flow of blood to the rest of the body in a slow, and silent way. Jeanette is telling my grandmother it is not her fault that Apa Chele died, and there is nothing she could've done to save him.

26.

You must manage to control what suddenly turns up. To struggle against a force that sweeps through and that you must pin down or else have it go beyond you and get lost.

Marguerite Duras, *Green Eyes*

July 2001. I want to vomit. "I don't feel very well," I say sheepishly as I stare out at the skeletal landscape. Even the desert wants to hide from itself. I want C to stop the car. I'm convinced that if I step outside, the discomfort of the heat will feel like a salve. In the parking lot of my sister's funeral, I lift my ten-year-old head to the sky and let the sun kiss my face. In that moment I am free. In this moment I am afraid. I am afraid that I've gotten myself into a bit of a situation. I'm in way over my head. This is unsustainable. I think there is something wrong with me because I will never be as happy, optimistic, cheerful, and sensitive as my un-medicated bipolar girlfriend.

Wide daily fluctuations started that summer, in the desert where there is no refuge. That C was painting large canvasses, writing poetry and plays, insisting on singing karaoke at the Holiday Inn, making jewelry, refinishing furniture, starting a hospice for cats, gardening, creating custom picture frames, experimenting with mixed media, practicing Bikram Yoga, napping at odd hours, and crying as quickly and briefly as a monsoon storm did not seem to give us pause. I learned later that manic and depressive symptoms may occur together or quickly one after the other in what is called a mixed state.

But months later, when it is finally over, it rains in Los Angeles for four days and four nights. The apartment feels violated, ransacked. I got rid of my crap when she moved in because I'm good at that and now I have nothing, again. I prefer it that way. My neighbor and friend, Deirdre Lewis (whom I call Mama D) and her kids sit on my empty floor with my new puppy Georgia filling the void. They will save me with their everyday come-and-go. Mama D uses my washer and dryer, and I pick up tiny underwear I randomly find on the hallway floor; I drop off candy valentines at Gardner Elementary because Darla forgot them on the steps; I pick up Harris from school because he's thrown up; I help Darla with her homework by showing her how to look the stuff up on Google. I hang up karate uniforms that have been forgotten inside the dryer. I think of Harris every morning because his Spider-Man outfit hangs on the hamper for weeks. They don't know how much I need them. I need Deirdre to talk to every day when she's in and out with her laundry; I need Harris to lounge on my couch with Georgia practically sitting on his head. These activities give me purpose and make me feel like I'm a part of something larger than myself. The Lewis family will buttress my collapsing sense of self so that I begin the reconstruction phase. I paint the apartment, get new furniture, practice yoga, stop drinking, stop eating meat, work on my documentary, overhaul my screenplay and work on this book. Barbara reminds me in *Shoreline Series* that I will become myself, a swinging door:

When we finally become ourselves, we become a swinging door; that gray book told me, that sandbank told me. When the boss is sleeping, everyone is sleeping, that gray book told me, that hurry bird told me. Thus, we have some idea of time (a little past noon), and some idea of place (Playa la Misión), a little bit of heaven told me, an absolute independence told me.

Everything is changed. And I feel free.

27.

Where you've nothing else, construct ceremonies out of the air and breathe upon them.

Cormac McCarthy, *The Road*

In *The Tibetan Book of the Dead* (more accurately translated as *The Great Book of Natural Liberation Through Understanding in the Between,* Bardo thos grol chen mo), which was composed by the great adept Padma Sambhava in the late eighth century, the question is asked, "What is death?" In the popular imagination, death is a terminal state, a nothingness, an oblivion, a void that destroys life. Death is sought after by those in misery and feared by those who feel happy. But what is nothing? And if it's nothing, then how can it be defined? Steve Hagen says:

> Nothing is after all just nothing. It cannot be a place that resembles an idea of nothingness. A place involves area, or extension. It is defined by coordinates and boundaries. It is not nothing. It is room. Nothing has no room, nor can

anything be located within nothing. Nothing cannot have an inside or an outside. It cannot destroy, swallow, or terminate. As nothing, it can have no energy or effect. As nothing, it cannot be a thing, a realm, a state or anything. It is absolutely nothing to fear. It is nothing to hope for.

And yet we think of nothing as something. We think of it as we think of deep sleep even though there is no credible evidence to suggest that there is any such thing as nothingness after death. Then what is there?

However, reading *The Tibetan Book of the Dead* is often difficult while exercising. And it's hard to concentrate on death when your heart is beating wildly while climbing the steep thread at Runyon Canyon. I've decided to stop thinking so hard and begin a self-improvement program instead. My friend Daniela Greene says, "Sometimes the best way to the spirit is through the body, especially for you, Victoria." My program includes the hard stuff, like therapy, meditation, martial arts, and vegetarianism. I drive to Metzler's Violin Shop in Glendale and pick out a nice cello, a rent-to-own kind of thing, explaining in detail how I have absolutely no musical skill that I know of, and it would therefore be a waste of time to acquire a cello that I cannot afford. After all, this is a big experiment. For some reason, I include the story of my mother buying me a guitar in the 6th grade, and although I loved taking guitar lessons, I could not sit still long enough to make any progress. Now I can sit still, I tell them.

In another life, I want to be like the famous cellist, Jacqueline Du Pré, but without multiple sclerosis. I would live and work in Vienna as a professional musician. I would stroll down the…blanky blank and live in a flat with a view. I would eat fresh-baked bread, drink wine every day, not feel the need for exercise, and maybe I would smoke occasionally and ride a bike leisurely through town, leading a calm and serene life. Instead, I live in Los Angeles eating a vegetarian diet, hiking ninety minutes every morning with my dog, doing yoga, curbing the carbs, and driving my Volkswagen like it's a sports car.

Inside my notebook's front cover, is a quote from an interview of Jorie Graham by Deirdre Wenger in April 2008. Jorie reminds me to:

Walk, look, smell, taste, touch, listen. Get your body back. Try to make yourself use all your senses every day. Find the strange, not the weird but the mysterious. We all need to work on staying awake. This is a somnolent era. Growing moreso. We need to work hard pretty much all the time, to achieve moments of presence and wakefulness.

In various exercises, in my bewilderment, I tried to live like I knew what death was. At the age of ten and having no idea I would turn into the person I am today; I didn't know that presence was the key to my life. I also didn't know that I could simply have a conversation with anything (or anyone) that disturbed my peace of mind. So, one morning, I poach some eggs and make a salad of arugula and tomatoes with a dash of fresh lemons from Judy's lemon tree. You can do this in California, just pick lemons off your neighbor's tree. I whip everything up while still in my pajamas and talk to Death about life. "We won't be staying," Death says while ungratefully devouring the free meal, "but I'll tell you what I can do. I can make your death accidental, a freakish thing that happens, nothing horrible, just a plain old accident on an ordinary warm spring day. No one will see it coming. Trust me, it's easier that way, for everyone."

July 2012. Los Angeles, CA. I decide to explore.

It all started when I decided to take my medicine. I had already been seeing my therapist and meditation teacher, Tanda, and I felt I was making incredible progress on my self-imposed, self-improvement program. I stare at the medicine placed delicately inside a small seashell by Daniela and Jamie, and silently state my intentions for my first plant ceremony. I say to the medicine, "I'm going to take you through my mouth, and you will flow through my bloodstream and untangle my protected heart. "Rest your head on me," says the medicine to the mind, "it's time for you to take a big break." The medicine takes me and breaks me and puts me back together like the new puzzle I want to be. "I will see you more than once," says the medicine plant to the human animal. "I will see you clearly in the light of the garden and you will come to me after I've left you. You will come to me again and again so that someday, you will remember who you really are." Thus, began my work with plants. I will visit my childhood wound in one manner or another consistently and without pause until the day the plants show me that I am done.

I decide to lean into this as a way of life. I travel to Costa Rica to do a juice cleanse and yoga retreat and there I meet a new friend Erin, who happens to be from Los Angeles and has trained with Shamans in Peru. All the pieces of my internal puzzle will start to come together. Erin introduces me to the sweat lodge, Jamie and Daniela guide my experience with sacred plants, and Tanda will help me unravel cords that lead to blind spots in my personal architecture. And then one day, I will meet Lisa—my personal kaleidoscope, a force of nature who will show me what sacred love feels like. It will be the beginning of a whole other story, born from serious inquiry and a curious thirst for truth. I feel as if I've arrived on another playing field and not only am I every single player, but I'm also the umpire of my own game.

28.

I lived in the present, which was
that part of the future you could see.
The past floated above my head,
like the sun and moon, visible but never reachable.

Louise Gluck, *Averno*

Shortly after the death of the girls, my mother invited the woman who
killed them over to speak with our families. No one could believe it.
My mother believed that it would be most beneficial to everyone if we
did not direct our anger at the woman responsible for the accident.
She believed that if we had a chance to meet this very human woman,
our hearts would forgive her, and compassion would prevail. My
mother, a woman of correct action makes ceremony out of life. Her
actions are so closely aligned with her beliefs that to her, inviting this
woman to speak to our family seemed an obvious decision, an
absolute necessity if we were going to heal. What remained more
amazing than my mother inviting this woman to speak with our
families was that this woman accepted the invitation.

Mrs. Meinert is sixty-plus years old. She has white hair that's teased up in a soft, short beehive and wears glasses, held to her head with a gold chain. She has the courage to stand in front of six crying children and a handful of adults to say, "I'm so sorry. I will live the rest of my life with the sorrow and the sadness that I have caused your family. Not a day will go by when I won't think of what I've done." Sitting there, barely able to watch her speak, my heart grows soft and expands, and I feel so bad for her. I feel so sorry for the burden this woman will have to bear that I momentarily forget that my sister is dead because this woman had too many gin and tonics at bridge club. I'm so grateful to Mrs. Meinert for giving me a moment of forgetting. It will remain one of the greatest gifts my mother bestowed on our family, the gift of showing us a way to forgive. I will understand in that moment that forgiveness is difficult when it really matters. I grow up believing you always have a choice to make the better decision. My mother could have left me. It happens. A parent loses a child, and they cannot fully recover enough to help the other one grow up. My mother never left me. And as for my father, he went away for a long time and then decided to come back to me.

June 2012. I am having lunch with the Dalai Lama and he tells me again that happiness is not something ready-made. It comes from our own actions. I wake up and my dog is sitting there, with her beautiful smile—already happy. While hiking Elysian Park I realize how much time I've had to think—like thirty years or so. I begin to imagine not having lost anything at all. Did Gina ever really exist? I read torturous books and feel the wounded aches of being in love and then not, and I think myself lucky to be. Just be. The drama of real-life seeps in and makes me feel lucky that she died on a day when she was happy. That nothing cold and unforgivable happened to her like I read in the newspapers or see on television or read in books. I arrive a different person, an arriviste in the world I've made for myself, and my old self is leery of this new interloper who wants to know more and who's feeling free and more powerful than ever before.

All the great wisdom traditions all over the world are in essential agreement that the actual moment of death is an extremely important and precious opportunity. In the *Essential Ken Wilber*, Wilber maintains that:

> If you at all believe that some part of you partakes of the divine, if you at all believe that you have access to some sort of Spirit that transcends your mortal body in any sense, then the moment of death is crucial, because at that point the mortal body is gone, and if there is anything that remains, this is the time to find out, yes?

As a young person, I can easily slip into the present moment. I am capable of walking into a parking lot at my sister's funeral and for a short moment, I feel like the person I was before she died, a girl with a sunshiny future. The sun on my face tells me with certainty that I'm going to be fine because at that moment, in the parking lot, next to the field, I am. People assume unless they've experienced it, that the funeral is the climactic part. It's not. The climactic part is the void of the loved one who has disappeared, except that it's not climactic in any way that an observer would notice. It's the daily absence that creates a gulf inside you, a space that is filled with emptiness. Until one day the emptiness starts filling up with feelings—and no matter how many feelings I let myself have, there is this small, tiny flame deep in the core of me that outshines the rest, and I attract to myself those people and moments when the flame can be stoked, made larger and hotter until I just catch on fire.

29.

Out behind ideas of
wrongdoing and rightdoing,
there is a field. I'll meet you
there.

When the soul lies down in
that grass,
the world is too full to talk
about.
Ideas, language, even the
phrase 'each other'
doesn't make any sense.

Rumi

Look at me! I'm flying above Pickle Road, and I swing low and fast
and just as I'm about to hit the dirt where they lay crooked, I swoop
up, barely missing, and I turn my head to look back down, and they

are all there. The cool black truck, the field, those people, my family who've had the unfortunate luck to be stuck in this awful moment, screaming, bewildered, and frightened, and me flying above them, watching it all happen with such ease as if these are the things that happen to people, all people, my people. Right now, is no different from later is no different from next year. Right now, I'm flying. Look at me, I'm up here, I scream. I'm possessed with the all-seeing wisdom of Athena riding as a mighty bird. I swoop, plummeting towards the earth, and I can see everything, the tiniest heartbeats, and the tiniest tears. I'm here. Look at me! Look up! I'm right here, with you! I circle again and again and again. I try to crash myself near her, but at the last minute, I brake and swing up. I can't do it. I can't kill myself. The life inside my heart won't let me. They die by themselves but I'm too afraid. I want to live.

I decide I will be more like you. I feel you watching me spin in circles, exhausting myself, having to be the best at everything. You clap for me and cheer for me while you sit on the grass, relaxing and eating an orange. Tell me about your life, please. I will tell you about mine. I will tell you how much I've missed you and how often I think of you. How much I've learned. How much you've taught me. How bad I feel that I wasn't there with you. I will tell you secrets that you already know because you know me like no other. I will tell you that I want true love, I want to earn more money, make a difference in the world, take walks with you, and you will giggle and tell me that I am what I want already and that I have what I need, and that true love is mine because I am true. And you love me as I am because that's what you do. I want to tell you face to face that I love you.

Stars hit my eyes and make me blind. Beth Alvarado reminds me, "That's what stars do when you are little, they make you think about light lost in the universe, about time, about your younger sister, asleep beside you. She was small then and the only one you loved fiercely."

I am walking down a long dirt Texas road towards you, but the road is too long, it never ends, and I never reach you. After some time, you turn to go, and I scream for you not to. I run as fast as I can to catch you, but you turn and smile, then you are gone. I keep running. And I keep running. I run until I have no energy left and I slump down in tears. The sun is setting on the horizon; it's suspended there but it doesn't go down. I watch it, waiting. I am of this, all of this. If I can be of this, then I am of everything. If ever I forget how much I love you, I will disappear. When I can no longer weep, I pick myself up and keep walking asking, how does the world not end? I am yours. You are mine.

It doesn't end because we belong to one another.

Works Cited

Ackerman, Diane. *Alchemy of the Mind*, Scribner, 2004, page 190.

Adorno, Theodor and Horkeimer, Max. *Verso/NLB*, 1997, page 120.

Carson, Anne. *Decreation: Poetry, Essays, Opera*, Random House Inc., 2006, page 107.

Carson, Anne. *Glass, Irony and God*, New Directions, 1995.

Chang, Larry, *Wisdom for the Soul: Five Millennia of Prescriptions for Spiritual Healing*, Gnosophia Publishers, 2006, page 735.

Coluccio, Felix. *Dictioinario Folklorico Argentino*, Rubén Darío Gasparini, Contributor Susana B Coluccio, Edition: 10, 2006.

Cully, Barbara, "Three Views of a Sunset in March." *Bayou*, 2009.

Cully, Barbara, *Shoreline Series.* Kore Press, 1997.

Deppman, Jed, Noble, Marianne, Stonum, Gary Lee, *Emily Dickinson and Philosophy*, 2013, page 182.

Diashonin, *Gosho Zenshu*, page 1598.

Dickinson, Emily, Poem: 835, *The Complete Poems of Emily Dickinson*, 1955.

Duras, Marguerite. *Writing*, translated by Mark Polizzotti, Lumen Editions, 1993, page 50.

Galeano, Eduardo. *Century of the Wind, Memory of Fire*, Vol. 3, translated by Cedric Belfrage, Open Road, New York, page 147.
Genevieve Jurgensen, *The Disappearance*, translated by Adriana Hunter, W.W. Norton & Co., 1999, page 29.

Gluck, Louise. *Averno*, Farrar, Straus and Giroux, 2007, page 42.

Graham, Jorie. Interview with Deirdre Wenger, April, 2008.

Chang, Larry, *Wisdom for the Soul: Five Millennia of Prescriptions for Spiritual Healing*, Gnosophia Publishers, 2006, page 735.

Hammad, Suheir. "Zeitoun," *Born Palestinian, Born Black*, Upset Press Inc. 2010, page 92.

Hammarskjöld, Dag. *Markings*, Random House, 1993.

Hagen, Steve. *Buddhism is Not What You Think: Finding Freedom Beyond Beliefs*, Harper Collins, 2003.

Issa, Kobayashi. *The Essentail Haiku*, translated by Robert Hass, 1994.

Lewis, M.D, Thomas, Amini, M.D., Fari, Lannon M.D, Richard, *A General Theory of Love*, 2000, page 15.

Marguerite Duras, *Green Eyes*, translated by Carol Barko, Columbia University Press, 1990.

Marcel Proust, *Swann's Way,* translated by Lydia Davis, Penguin
Classics, November 30, 2004

Mayo Foundation for Medical Education and Research (MFMER)
©1998-2008.

McCarthy, Cormac. *The Road,* Vintage Bookays, 2006, page 74.

Miller, Jane. *Midnights, an Essay,* University Press of New
England, Jan 31, 2008.

Mitchell, W.J.T. *What Do Pictures Want? The Lives and Loves of
Images,* as published in Art in America, 2004.

Moffatt, James. Epistle of James 1:16-17, *The General Epistles,
James, Peter and Judas,* 1947.

Neruda, Pablo. *Residence on Earth: Poems,* translated by Donald D.
Walsh, New Directions Bookays, 2004

Nye, Naomi Shihab. "The Art of Disappearing," *Words Under the
Words: Selected Poems,* Far Corner Books, 1995.

Paz, Octavio. *The Tradition, a Tale of Two Gardens: Poems from
India,* edited by Eliot Weinberger, A New Directions Bibelot,
1997, page 63.

Rainer Maria Rilke, *Letters to a Young Poet,* #7,

Rickel, Boyer. "On Consciousness," Cue, A Journal of Prose Poetry,
2006, Volume 3, Issue 2, page 24.

Rosmarie Waldrop, *The Reproduction of Profiles*, 1984, page 63.

Rowe, David E. And Schulmann, Robert J., *The Goal of Human Existence*, Princeton University Press, Einstein Archives, 11 April 1943, 2007, 28-587.

Sante, Luc. *Evidence, NYPD Crime Scene Photographs: 1914-1918*, 2006, page 61.

Shakespeare, William. *The Complete Works of Shakespeare*, David Bevington, fourth edition, 1622 Sonnets #28.

Sontag, Susan. *Regarding the Pain of Others*, Picador, 2003, page 60.

Stephen Jay Gould, *The Panda's Thumb*, W.W. Norton & Company, Inc., 1980, page 28.

St. Teresa of Avila, *The Collected Works of St. Teresa of Avila*, Vol. 1, Institute of Carmelite Studies, 1980.

St. Teresa of Avila. *The Four Waters*, www. Ocarm.org 2003-2015.

St. Teresa of Avila. *L'Osservatore Romano*, English edition, November 9, 1981.

Swami Paramananda, *The Upanishads*, The Floating Press, 1919, page 64.

Tagore, Rabindranath. *Sadhana*, Doubleday, 2004, pages 73 and 88.

The History Place, Genocide in the 20ᵗʰ Century, historyplace.com, 1999.

Thurman, A.F., *The Tibetan Book of the Dead*, translated, page 20.

Tomas Abraham, Tomas, Russovich, Alejandro and Mari, Enrique, *The Destiny of Borges*, translated by Jennifer Acker, Harpers, April, 2008.

Weyl, Herman. *The Philosophy of Mathematics and Natural Science*, Princeton University Press, Princeton 1950.

Wilber, Ken. *The Essential Ken Wilber: Sex, Ecology, and Spirituality*, Shambhala, 1998.

Acknowledgments

With my deepest appreciation, I would like to thank Barbara Cully—without your devotion to my story, your patience, love and encouragement, this book would have remained a word doc in the belly of my computer. To Beth Alvarado, for your thoughtful editorial feedback which was always in the service of this book and for that, I am forever grateful.

I would like to thank my mother, Maria Teresa Garza, who taught me about the importance of the pursuit as much as the achievement. I would like to thank my father, Jesse Garza, for making me feel special and reminding me to enjoy life. I would like to thank my other family members who willingly offered me their memorias for this project; Emilia Resendez, Patricia Resendez, Margarita Rodriguez, Peggy TenEyck, and Rachel Salas. I would like to thank Manuel Rodriguez for his love and kindness while I was growing up. I would like to thank the other women in my family; my Tía Eva Sifuentez for always pulling me onto her lap, despite my age; my Tía Maria Bowser for showing me the power of serving others without any fanfare; and finally, my Tía Lupita Villarreal whose strength of voice allowed me to believe that I deserve to say whatever I have to say to the world—thank you Tia, and Tio George for believing in me and helping me become a storyteller.

I would like to express my sincerest gratitude to Jane Miller, for showing me how to be an artist and for all my readers who offered their time and erudite suggestions in helping me get this book where it is today. Thank you from the bottom of my heart to Kim Westerman, Boyer Rickel, Valentyna Grenier, and Stef Willen. I would like to thank Jennifer Fisher for your bright mind to talk about all the real things. Thank you to Lesley Roberts for being my cheerleader and friend; Michelle Tountas, for making a home for me and offering me the gift of your unconditional friendship; Sage Guyton, and Weston Tountas for being the coolest cats on earth, I'm so lucky to know you. Deirdre, Darla, and Harry Lewis for cementing your beautiful selves in my heart; Michelle and Dallas Hallam for making our homestead in the city a true family experience. And to John and Colleen Cully for giving me the gift of their beach home in Mexico where I wrote most of this book.

I would like to thank Hedgebrook, for investing in me as a writer, and the unflagging support of everyone there. Thank you to my publisher Jen Harris and the whole team at JackLeg Press, for believing in this book and creating such a vibrant community of writers and book lovers.

Finally, and most importantly, I'd like to thank Lisa Garza. My steadfast source of inspiration and love, my biggest supporter and the truest expression of an authentic person that I know. You teach me always, and I am grateful every day that you picked me. Thank you for believing in me and in this book. Thank you to my sun and moon, Augustin and Dakota, you make being your mommy one of the greatest privileges of my life

JACKLEG PRESS

V. Joshua Adams, Scott Brown, Brittney Corrigan, Allison Cundiff, Jessica Cuello, Barbara Cully, Suzanne Frischkorn, Victoria Garza, Reginald Gibbons, D.C. Gonzales-Prieto, Neil de la Flor, Joachim Glage, Caroline Goodwin, Jennifer Harris, Meagan Lehr, Brigitte Lewis, Jean McGarry, D.K. McCutchen, Jenny Magnus, Rita Mookerjee, Mamie Morgan, cin salach, Jo Salas, Maureen Seaton, Kristine Snodgrass, Cornelia Maude Spelman, Peter Stenson, Hugh Behm-Steinberg, Melissa Studdard, Megan Weiler, David Wesley Williams

jacklegpress.org

CPSIA information can be obtained
at www.ICGtesting.com
Printed in the USA
BVHW042210191122
652367BV00005B/255

9 781737 513490